UNLOCKING BUSINESS SUCCESS

The Critical Role of HR KPIs

David M Arnold, MS, SPHR

Crystal Coast HR

Unlocking Business Success

Disclaimer

The information presented in this book is intended for educational and informational purposes only. While every effort has been made to ensure the accuracy and reliability of the content, the author and publisher do not guarantee the applicability or suitability of the information for your specific circumstances. This book is not a substitute for professional advice, and readers are encouraged to consult with qualified professionals in the fields of human resources, legal compliance, or business management for personalized guidance.

The concepts, strategies, and metrics discussed in this book are based on general principles and may not fully address unique organizational challenges or local regulatory requirements. Readers are responsible for conducting their own research and due diligence to ensure that the implementation of HR KPIs complies with applicable laws and aligns with their organizational values and goals.

The author and publisher disclaim any liability for damages or losses arising from the use or misuse of the information contained in this book. By reading this book, you acknowledge and agree to these terms.

The inclusion of references, examples, and case studies is for illustrative purposes only and does not imply endorsement or affiliation with any specific organizations, products, or services. All trademarks and copyrights mentioned in this book are the property of their respective owners.

Thank you for your understanding and for taking the time to explore the critical role of HR KPIs in shaping successful businesses.

Copyright

Copyright © [Year] [Your Name/Your Organization]. All rights reserved.

No part of this publication may be reproduced, distributed, or transmitted in any form or by any means, including photocopying, recording, or other electronic or mechanical methods, without the prior written permission of the publisher, except in the case of brief quotations embodied in critical reviews and certain other noncommercial uses permitted by copyright law.

For permission requests, write to the publisher at [Your Address] or contact via email at [Your Email Address].

The information provided in this book is for general informational purposes only and is protected under copyright law. Unauthorized use of this material is prohibited and may result in legal action. The author and publisher retain all rights to this material, including the right to update or revise the content as deemed necessary.

Acknowledgment

Creating this book has been an incredible journey, one that would not have been possible without the support and guidance of many individuals. First and foremost, I would like to express my deepest gratitude to my family and friends, whose unwavering belief in me provided the motivation to see this project through.

To my colleagues in the human resources field, thank you for inspiring me with your passion for improving workplace dynamics and for your invaluable contributions to the profession. Your insights and shared experiences have greatly influenced the perspectives presented in this book.

I am also grateful to the countless business leaders, HR professionals, and organizations who have shared their stories and lessons on implementing effective KPIs. Your real-world applications and successes have added depth and authenticity to this work.

A heartfelt thank you to my editor and publishing team for their meticulous attention to detail and for bringing this vision to life. Your expertise and guidance have been instrumental in shaping this book into a resource I am proud to share.

Lastly, I want to thank you, the reader, for your interest in exploring the critical role of HR KPIs in business success. It is my hope that this book serves as a valuable tool in your jour

Dedication

To those who inspire growth and perseverance, to the dreamers, the doers, and the believers — this work is for you. May it serve as a reminder that every step, no matter how small, brings us closer to becoming the best version of ourselves. Thank you for your unwavering support, guidance, and belief in what we can achieve together.

Table of Contents

Disclaimer 2
Copyright 3
Acknowledgment 4
Dedication 5
Preface 8
Introduction: Understanding the Role of HR KPIs in Business Health 10
Chapter 1: Defining HR KPIs and Their Purpose 17
Chapter 2: Aligning HR KPIs with Organizational Goals 25
Chapter 3: Key HR KPIs Every Business Should Track 34
Chapter 4: Measuring Employee Engagement and Satisfaction 45
Chapter 5: Enhancing Recruitment and Retention through HR KPIs 55
Chapter 6: Assessing Learning and Development through KPIs 65
Chapter 7: Understanding the Impact of Compensation and Benefits KPIs 76
Chapter 8: Driving Diversity and Inclusion with HR KPIs 87
Chapter 9: The Role of HR KPIs in Business Strategy and Decision-Making 97
Chapter 10: Using HR KPIs for Continuous Improvement and Adaptation 106
Chapter 11: Common Challenges in Implementing HR KPIs and How to Overcome Them 113
Chapter 12: Future Trends: The Evolving Role of HR KPIs in Business Health 119

Conclusion: The Critical Role of HR KPIs in Shaping a Successful Business 127

Appendix: 40 KPIs 133

Preface

In the dynamic world of business, human resources (HR) has transitioned from being a mere administrative function to a strategic partner integral to organizational success. The evolution of HR has brought with it the recognition that data-driven decision-making is no longer optional—it is essential. This book, "Unlocking Business Success: The Critical Role of HR KPIs," is a culmination of insights, strategies, and practical applications aimed at empowering business leaders and HR professionals to harness the full potential of HR Key Performance Indicators (KPIs).

The idea for this book stemmed from a simple yet profound observation: businesses that prioritize their people thrive in the long term. But how do organizations measure the effectiveness of their people-related strategies? How do they ensure that their HR initiatives align with broader business goals? The answer lies in HR KPIs. These metrics are not just numbers; they are the heartbeat of an organization, providing a real-time pulse on its health and vitality.

Throughout this book, we explore the multifaceted role of HR KPIs, delving into their significance, application, and impact on business strategy. Each chapter is designed to provide a comprehensive understanding of specific aspects of HR KPIs, from their definition and alignment with organizational goals to their role in recruitment, retention, employee engagement, diversity, and future trends.

This book is not just for HR professionals. It is for anyone invested in the success of their organization—CEOs, managers, team leaders, and even employees who want to understand how their contributions are measured and valued. By demystifying HR KPIs and providing actionable insights, this book aims to bridge the gap between data and decision-making, empowering readers to create workplaces that are not only productive but also inclusive, engaging, and future-ready.

As you embark on this journey through the chapters, I encourage you to think of HR KPIs not as rigid metrics but as tools for storytelling. Each KPI tells a story about your organization—its strengths, challenges, and opportunities. It is my hope that this book will inspire you to use these stories to drive positive change and build a foundation for sustainable success.

Welcome to a world where data meets strategy, where metrics become meaningful, and where HR KPIs unlock the true potential of your business. Let the journey begin.

Introduction: Understanding the Role of HR KPIs in Business Health

In today's competitive business environment, companies are increasingly looking for ways to maximize efficiency, drive employee satisfaction, and achieve their strategic goals. One of the most effective tools for measuring and improving business performance is Key Performance Indicators (KPIs), particularly those related to Human Resources (HR). HR KPIs serve as powerful metrics that provide insight into the effectiveness of a company's workforce and the overall health of its organizational structure.

This introductory chapter will explain the importance of HR KPIs in assessing the overall performance and health of a business. We will explore how these indicators act as a barometer for organizational efficiency, employee satisfaction, and strategic alignment. By setting the stage for the chapters that follow, we aim to illustrate how HR KPIs can be used to align HR practices with business objectives, ultimately driving business growth and sustainability.

What Are HR KPIs?

Human Resources Key Performance Indicators (HR KPIs) are quantifiable metrics that organizations use to assess and evaluate various aspects of their human resources practices. These indicators measure employee performance, engagement, satisfaction, retention, and various other factors that can directly impact an organization's success. By tracking and analyzing HR KPIs, businesses can gain valuable insights into how their workforce is performing and whether their HR strategies are achieving the desired results.

HR KPIs are tailored to the specific goals and objectives of a business. For example, an organization that focuses heavily on customer service might track KPIs related to employee performance and training, while a company in a fast-growth phase may prioritize metrics related to recruitment and retention. Regardless of the focus, HR KPIs allow businesses to take a data-driven approach to human capital management, ensuring that HR decisions are aligned with the company's strategic goals.

The Importance of HR KPIs in Business Health

HR KPIs are essential in understanding the overall health of an organization. Business health refers to an organization's ability to achieve its goals, sustain long-term growth, maintain operational efficiency, and adapt to changes in the market or workforce. To assess the health of a business, it is necessary to consider both the internal and external factors that contribute to its success. While financial performance is often the primary focus, the strength and efficiency of the workforce are equally important in determining a company's long-term viability.

Effective HR practices can lead to numerous benefits for businesses, including increased productivity, improved employee satisfaction, and reduced turnover. These outcomes, in turn, have a significant impact on profitability and overall business success. By tracking HR KPIs, companies can monitor the effectiveness of their HR strategies and adjust them as needed to ensure the business remains healthy and competitive.

Organizational Efficiency

Organizational efficiency is one of the core drivers of business health. In a competitive market, businesses need to maximize their resources, reduce waste, and streamline processes to remain profitable. HR KPIs play a critical role in assessing the efficiency of an organization's workforce. For example, KPIs such as time-to-fill, employee turnover rate, and productivity per employee can provide insights into how well an organization is utilizing its human resources.

High turnover rates, for instance, can be a sign of inefficiency in recruitment or employee engagement strategies. Similarly, if employees are not meeting performance expectations, it may indicate issues with training, motivation, or management. By regularly tracking these KPIs, businesses can identify areas where improvements are needed and take corrective actions to optimize workforce efficiency.

Employee Satisfaction

Employee satisfaction is another key component of organizational health. A satisfied workforce is more likely to be engaged, productive, and loyal, which directly contributes to a company's success. HR KPIs related to employee satisfaction, such as employee engagement scores, job satisfaction surveys, and Net Promoter Scores (NPS), provide organizations with valuable feedback on how employees perceive their roles and the company as a whole.

Understanding employee satisfaction levels allows businesses to identify potential areas of improvement, whether it's in the form of better benefits, improved work-life balance, or more opportunities for professional development. By addressing employee concerns and fostering a positive workplace culture, businesses can reduce turnover, improve morale, and ultimately increase productivity.

Strategic Alignment

HR KPIs also play a crucial role in ensuring that HR practices are aligned with the broader strategic goals of the organization. Strategic alignment refers to the process of ensuring that every department, team, and employee within the organization is working towards the same overarching objectives. HR strategies should support these goals by ensuring that the right talent is hired, developed, and retained to drive business success.

For example, if an organization's strategic goal is to expand into new markets, HR might focus on recruiting individuals with international experience or developing leadership programs to prepare employees for management roles in new regions. KPIs related to recruitment success, leadership development, and internal mobility can help businesses assess whether HR strategies are effectively contributing to the organization's strategic goals.

By measuring HR KPIs, businesses can track the alignment of their workforce with the company's strategic vision and make adjustments to HR policies or initiatives as needed to support long-term objectives. Without this alignment, HR efforts may be misdirected, leading to wasted resources, unfulfilled goals, and missed opportunities for growth.

The Role of Data in HR KPIs

One of the primary advantages of HR KPIs is the ability to make data-driven decisions. In the past, HR departments relied heavily on intuition and anecdotal evidence to guide decision-making. However, with the advent of advanced analytics and HR technology, businesses now have access to a wealth of data that can be used to measure and improve HR performance.

For example, through data analysis, businesses can uncover trends in employee turnover, identify the causes of high absenteeism, or assess the effectiveness of training programs. This data allows HR professionals to make more informed decisions about where to allocate resources and how to improve the organization's overall workforce strategy.

HR KPIs provide an objective, measurable way to track progress toward key business objectives. Rather than relying on subjective impressions or opinions, HR KPIs offer concrete evidence that can help leaders make smarter decisions, reduce costs, and improve operational efficiency.

Using HR KPIs for Continuous Improvement

HR KPIs are not just about measuring success; they are also about driving continuous improvement. By tracking KPIs over time, businesses can identify patterns and trends that provide valuable insights into areas of strength and areas that need improvement.

For example, if an organization notices that its employee turnover rate has been steadily increasing over the past few months, it can use this data to investigate potential causes, such as poor management, low employee engagement, or insufficient compensation. By identifying these issues early, businesses can take proactive steps to address them, whether it's by implementing new training programs, offering more competitive benefits, or improving communication and feedback processes.

Continuous improvement is a key tenet of successful organizations, and HR KPIs provide the tools needed to make ongoing adjustments that enhance the business's health and performance.

The Challenges of Implementing HR KPIs

While HR KPIs provide valuable insights into business health, it's important to acknowledge that implementing these metrics can be challenging. For one, HR professionals must ensure that the data they are collecting is accurate and reliable. Inaccurate or incomplete data can lead to misleading conclusions, which may result in poor decision-making.

Additionally, organizations may face resistance to change from employees or management when introducing new HR metrics or performance measures. Overcoming this resistance and creating a culture of data-driven decision-making requires clear communication and buy-in from all levels of the organization.

Despite these challenges, the benefits of using HR KPIs far outweigh the obstacles. By setting clear goals, continuously measuring performance, and making data-driven decisions, businesses can improve employee satisfaction, increase productivity, and achieve long-term strategic success.

Conclusion: Setting the Stage for HR KPIs in Business Health

HR KPIs play a crucial role in measuring and maintaining the overall health of a business. They serve as a powerful tool for assessing organizational efficiency, employee satisfaction, and strategic alignment. By tracking and analyzing these metrics, companies can ensure that their HR strategies are contributing to business success and that their workforce is engaged, productive, and aligned with the company's goals.

The chapters that follow will delve deeper into the specific HR KPIs that businesses should track and how they can use these metrics to drive performance and growth. By understanding and implementing effective HR KPIs, businesses can create a foundation for continuous improvement, greater operational efficiency, and long-term success.

In the next chapter, we will define HR KPIs in greater detail, explain their purpose, and begin exploring the key HR metrics that every organization should measure to ensure the health of their workforce and the success of their business.

Chapter 1: Defining HR KPIs and Their Purpose

In the complex and fast-evolving landscape of modern business, human resources (HR) play a pivotal role in driving organizational success. To ensure that HR practices are aligned with business goals, organizations use a range of tools, and one of the most important among them is Key Performance Indicators (KPIs). This chapter delves into the fundamentals of HR KPIs, providing a thorough understanding of what they are, their purpose, and how they contribute to overall business performance.

What Are HR KPIs?

Key Performance Indicators (KPIs) are measurable values that indicate how effectively an individual, team, or organization is achieving key objectives. KPIs can be used to measure performance in almost every area of a business, but in the context of Human Resources, they are focused on the workforce and how well HR functions are contributing to the success of the company. HR KPIs are quantifiable metrics that help HR professionals and business leaders track the effectiveness of their human resources practices, such as recruitment, retention, training, engagement, and performance management.

The term "KPI" itself may seem simple, but its application in HR is multifaceted. At their core, HR KPIs are designed to measure outcomes that directly impact the performance of the organization's workforce, which in turn affects the broader goals of the business. HR KPIs typically fall under several key categories, including employee productivity, retention, satisfaction, and talent acquisition. However, they can be customized to reflect the specific needs and goals of the organization.

The Purpose of HR KPIs

The primary purpose of HR KPIs is to help businesses assess how well their HR strategies are functioning and whether they are aligned with the organization's broader business goals. In a nutshell, HR KPIs are designed to answer a fundamental question: **Are the people driving the organization's success being effectively managed and supported?**

Measuring HR-related factors is crucial to overall business success for several reasons:

1. **Alignment with Business Goals**: HR is no longer just about hiring, training, and paying employees—it's about aligning the workforce with the organization's strategic objectives. KPIs provide a clear way to measure how well HR practices support organizational goals such as growth, profitability, and sustainability. For example, if a business goal is to

expand into new markets, HR KPIs related to talent acquisition and leadership development can help determine whether the workforce is prepared to meet this objective.

2. **Operational Efficiency**: Business leaders need to know that they are making the most of their human capital. HR KPIs allow organizations to measure efficiency in processes like recruitment, onboarding, training, and performance management. By measuring KPIs such as time-to-fill positions or cost-per-hire, HR departments can identify inefficiencies and streamline processes to save time and money.

3. **Employee Satisfaction and Engagement**: A motivated and satisfied workforce is essential to achieving business goals. HR KPIs that focus on employee satisfaction, engagement, and retention provide organizations with insights into the overall mood and well-being of their employees. These metrics help identify areas where improvements can be made in employee experience, company culture, and leadership effectiveness.

4. **Risk Mitigation**: HR KPIs can help identify potential risks that could affect the health of the organization. For example, a high turnover rate or a low employee engagement score can be early indicators of underlying issues in the workplace. By tracking these KPIs, businesses can proactively address problems before they become serious, thereby mitigating potential risks to productivity and morale.

5. **Strategic Decision-Making**: HR KPIs provide data that can inform decision-making across the business. Rather than relying on intuition or anecdotal evidence,

business leaders can use KPIs to make decisions based on hard data. For example, a business may use turnover data to decide whether to adjust compensation packages, implement new retention strategies, or improve leadership development programs.

6. **Continuous Improvement**: One of the most powerful aspects of HR KPIs is their ability to drive continuous improvement. By tracking KPIs over time, HR departments can identify patterns, trends, and areas of improvement. This allows businesses to refine their HR practices, increase efficiency, and enhance employee engagement over the long term.

HR KPIs vs. Other Types of Performance Metrics

While HR KPIs are an essential tool for measuring workforce effectiveness, it is important to distinguish them from other types of performance metrics used in business. Many organizations track financial metrics, operational KPIs, and customer-related metrics to gauge overall performance, but HR KPIs are unique in that they focus specifically on the people side of the business.

1. **Financial Metrics**: Financial KPIs measure aspects like profitability, revenue, and cost efficiency. While these metrics are critical to understanding the financial health of a business, they do not provide insights into how effectively an organization is managing its human capital. For example, while financial metrics like profit margins or return on investment (ROI) are important, they don't capture the underlying factors that drive business success, such as employee performance or engagement. HR KPIs

complement financial metrics by adding a human element to business performance.

2. **Operational KPIs**: Operational KPIs measure the efficiency and effectiveness of business processes, such as production, supply chain management, or customer service. While operational KPIs focus on tangible outputs and processes, HR KPIs focus on the performance of the workforce and how human capital is being utilized to achieve those operational goals. HR KPIs are therefore an essential complement to operational KPIs because they provide insight into how well the workforce is contributing to operational efficiency.

3. **Customer KPIs**: Customer-related KPIs, such as customer satisfaction, Net Promoter Score (NPS), and customer retention, measure how well a business is meeting customer needs. While customer KPIs are vital for understanding market success, HR KPIs focus on the internal factors—such as employee training, performance, and engagement—that contribute to customer experience. A highly engaged and well-trained workforce is often the driving force behind customer satisfaction, which is why HR KPIs are crucial for improving customer-related outcomes.

4. **Sales and Marketing KPIs**: These KPIs track the effectiveness of sales and marketing activities, such as lead conversion rates, customer acquisition costs, and sales growth. While these metrics are essential for measuring the success of revenue-generating activities, HR KPIs focus on the internal processes and people that enable the sales and marketing teams to perform at their best. For example, measuring the performance of salespeople or evaluating the

effectiveness of sales training programs can be tracked using HR KPIs.

How HR KPIs Align with Business Objectives

HR KPIs are essential in ensuring that human resources are working toward the same goals as the rest of the organization. In order for a business to thrive, its HR function must align closely with the company's strategic objectives. This alignment ensures that HR efforts are focused on building and maintaining a workforce that supports business growth, profitability, and long-term sustainability.

Strategic Workforce Planning

Strategic workforce planning is one of the key areas where HR KPIs play an essential role. HR KPIs help organizations understand the current state of their workforce and make decisions about future talent needs. For example, KPIs such as turnover rate, hiring rate, and talent pipeline health allow businesses to plan for future workforce requirements and ensure that the right skills are available to meet business demands.

If a business has aggressive growth goals or plans to expand into new markets, HR can use KPIs to assess whether the current workforce is equipped to handle these changes. Additionally, HR KPIs like employee training and development completion rates help organizations determine whether their employees have the necessary skills to adapt to new business requirements.

Driving Performance and Productivity

HR KPIs help track individual and team performance, ensuring that employees are contributing effectively to business objectives. KPIs such as employee performance reviews, goal achievement, and productivity metrics allow managers to assess whether employees are meeting performance expectations and how they can improve.

By setting clear performance targets and tracking them over time, organizations can identify high performers, reward top talent, and provide development opportunities for underperforming employees. HR KPIs allow businesses to ensure that their workforce is performing at its highest potential, directly impacting overall business success.

Talent Acquisition and Retention

An organization's ability to attract, recruit, and retain top talent is directly linked to its long-term success. HR KPIs that measure recruitment efficiency, such as time-to-fill, cost-per-hire, and applicant quality, help businesses assess the effectiveness of their hiring strategies. Similarly, KPIs that track retention, such as employee turnover rates and exit interview feedback, provide insights into whether the company is successfully retaining key employees.

In a competitive labor market, businesses must continuously refine their talent acquisition and retention strategies. HR KPIs allow businesses to track progress in these areas and adjust their approach to ensure that they are attracting and retaining the best talent available.

Conclusion

HR KPIs are essential tools for any organization looking to optimize its workforce and align HR practices with broader business objectives. They provide data-driven insights into the effectiveness of HR strategies, helping businesses drive efficiency, enhance employee satisfaction, and mitigate potential risks. By measuring HR-related factors such as recruitment, retention, performance, and engagement, businesses can make informed decisions that ultimately lead to improved business performance and long-term success.

In the following chapters, we will explore specific HR KPIs in greater detail and discuss how they can be used to address key business challenges and improve organizational health. By understanding the importance and purpose of HR KPIs, organizations can develop a more strategic approach to human capital management, ensuring that they are well-positioned to achieve their goals in an increasingly competitive business landscape.

Chapter 2: Aligning HR KPIs with Organizational Goals

In today's fast-paced and highly competitive business environment, human resources (HR) functions are increasingly seen as a strategic partner in driving organizational success. The days when HR was primarily concerned with administrative tasks like payroll and benefits are long gone. Now, HR plays a crucial role in shaping and executing business strategies. To achieve this, HR departments must not only ensure that day-to-day operations run smoothly but also align their activities with the broader organizational goals. One of the key tools for ensuring this alignment is Key Performance Indicators (KPIs).

This chapter explores the critical concept of aligning HR KPIs with organizational goals, focusing on how specific HR functions such as talent acquisition, employee engagement, training, and retention can directly influence key business outcomes. By understanding this alignment, HR departments can demonstrate their value, drive measurable results, and contribute to the overall health and success of the organization.

The Importance of Alignment Between HR KPIs and Organizational Goals

Before delving into the specific ways HR KPIs align with organizational goals, it's important to understand why this alignment is crucial for business success. Every organization, regardless of industry, has certain objectives that it aims to achieve. These objectives might include increasing profitability, enhancing customer satisfaction, expanding market share, or improving operational efficiency. In today's knowledge economy, a well-trained and engaged workforce is a key driver of these business goals.

Without proper alignment between HR KPIs and organizational objectives, businesses risk operating in silos. HR functions may pursue goals that are disconnected from the needs of the broader organization, resulting in inefficiencies, low employee morale, and missed opportunities. Moreover, an unaligned HR department may fail to provide the necessary support for achieving key business outcomes such as growth, profitability, and market leadership.

When HR KPIs are carefully aligned with organizational goals, however, HR can act as a catalyst for achieving these objectives. Aligning HR metrics with business outcomes ensures that HR efforts contribute to the company's broader vision. For example, if a company aims to increase profitability, HR KPIs related to employee productivity, retention, and performance management can help ensure that the workforce is operating at its highest potential.

Key HR Functions and Their Role in Organizational Goals

To effectively align HR KPIs with organizational objectives, it's essential to understand how different HR functions impact key business outcomes. Below, we will explore four of the most critical HR functions—talent acquisition, employee engagement, training and development, and retention—and examine how HR KPIs related to these functions can directly influence the broader goals of the business.

Talent Acquisition: Attracting the Right Talent

One of the most important functions of HR is talent acquisition. The ability to attract and hire the right talent is fundamental to the success of any business. Having the right people in the right roles is a key driver of productivity, profitability, and long-term growth. For HR departments, measuring the effectiveness of their talent acquisition processes is vital in aligning with organizational goals.

HR KPIs in Talent Acquisition: Several HR KPIs are crucial in evaluating the effectiveness of talent acquisition strategies, including:

- **Time-to-Fill**: This KPI measures the amount of time it takes from the moment a job is posted until a candidate is hired. The shorter the time-to-fill, the more efficiently the recruitment process is functioning. For businesses aiming to maintain or accelerate growth, a low time-to-fill is essential to ensuring that critical positions are filled quickly, enabling the company to respond to new opportunities.

- **Cost-per-Hire**: This metric calculates the total cost involved in hiring a new employee, including advertising, recruiter fees, and interview expenses. For businesses looking to improve profitability, reducing the cost-per-hire without compromising the quality of candidates is essential.

- **Quality of Hire**: Measuring the success of new hires based on their performance, cultural fit, and longevity within the company is another critical KPI. High-quality hires contribute to organizational success by boosting productivity and reducing turnover.

By aligning these talent acquisition KPIs with organizational goals such as growth, profitability, and market expansion, HR can ensure that the recruitment process is driving the success of the business.

Employee Engagement: Driving Motivation and Productivity

Employee engagement is another critical factor that directly influences business performance. Engaged employees are more motivated, productive, and committed to the company's mission, while disengaged employees are more likely to underperform or leave the organization altogether. Aligning employee engagement strategies with broader business goals ensures that employees are working toward common objectives, leading to higher levels of performance and business success.

HR KPIs in Employee Engagement: There are several KPIs that measure employee engagement, including:

- **Employee Engagement Scores**: Often measured through surveys, this KPI evaluates how employees feel about their work, their relationship with leadership, and the company culture. High engagement scores are indicative of a motivated and satisfied workforce, which translates to higher productivity and job satisfaction.

- **Employee Net Promoter Score (eNPS):** The eNPS measures the likelihood that employees would recommend the company to others as a great place to work. A high eNPS score reflects strong engagement and satisfaction, which can lead to improved retention and a better employer brand.

- **Absenteeism Rate:** A high absenteeism rate can indicate low employee engagement or dissatisfaction. Conversely, a low absenteeism rate suggests a healthy work environment where employees are motivated to come to work regularly, leading to higher productivity.

Aligning employee engagement KPIs with organizational goals such as improved performance, retention, and customer satisfaction allows HR to focus on strategies that enhance motivation, build a positive work culture, and contribute to the business's overall success.

Training and Development: Upskilling for Growth

Continuous learning and development are critical to ensuring that employees have the skills and knowledge needed to perform their jobs effectively and grow with the organization. Investing in training programs not only enhances employee productivity but also supports long-term business goals such as innovation, customer satisfaction, and market competitiveness.

HR KPIs in Training and Development: Several KPIs measure the effectiveness of training and development programs, including:

- **Training Completion Rate:** This KPI measures the percentage of employees who complete their assigned training programs. A high completion rate indicates that employees are engaged in their development, which can directly impact their productivity and job performance.

- **Training Effectiveness:** This can be measured through post-training assessments or surveys to determine how much knowledge or skills employees have gained from a program. Training programs that effectively enhance employee capabilities contribute to the overall goals of the business.

- **Employee Development Progress:** Tracking employees' progress in their development journey, such as promotions or job role changes, helps determine whether training and development programs are preparing employees for greater responsibilities within the company.

By aligning training KPIs with organizational objectives such as innovation, operational efficiency, or leadership development, HR can ensure that the workforce is equipped to meet the evolving needs of the business and stay competitive in the market.

Employee Retention: Reducing Turnover for Long-Term Success

Employee retention is one of the most significant challenges facing organizations today. High turnover rates can be costly, leading to lost productivity, additional recruitment costs, and a decrease in employee morale. As such, aligning retention strategies with organizational goals is crucial for ensuring a stable and motivated workforce that supports long-term growth.

HR KPIs in Employee Retention: Key retention KPIs include:

- **Employee Turnover Rate:**

    This measures the percentage of employees who leave the organization within a certain period. A high turnover rate can signal underlying problems with the work environment, leadership, or company culture, while a low turnover rate indicates a stable workforce.

- **Retention Rate:**

    This KPI calculates the percentage of employees who remain with the company over time. A high retention rate often correlates with employee satisfaction, engagement, and loyalty, all of which contribute to the long-term success of the business.

- **Exit Interviews:**

    Conducting exit interviews and tracking reasons for turnover provides valuable insights into why employees leave. This data can inform HR strategies to improve retention, which directly supports organizational goals such as reducing recruitment costs and maintaining a stable, experienced workforce.

Aligning retention KPIs with organizational goals, such as minimizing costs, improving performance, and enhancing company culture, helps ensure that HR is focusing on retaining top talent, which is vital for long-term business success.

The Role of HR in Business Strategy

When HR KPIs are aligned with organizational goals, HR can become a strategic partner in achieving those goals. This requires HR professionals to go beyond transactional HR tasks (like payroll and benefits administration) and play a more active role in the strategic decision-making process. HR professionals must be involved in discussions around company growth, innovation, and long-term planning to ensure that the workforce is prepared and able to support these objectives.

To align HR KPIs effectively, HR leaders must work closely with business leaders to understand the company's strategic priorities. For example, if the company is planning to expand into new markets, HR must ensure that the organization has the right talent in place to support this expansion. HR KPIs can provide the data needed to make decisions about recruitment, training, and workforce planning to support such initiatives.

Additionally, HR departments can use their insights from KPIs to forecast future workforce needs. If KPIs show that employee turnover is rising or that productivity levels are declining, HR can take proactive measures to address these issues, such as improving training programs or enhancing employee engagement efforts.

Conclusion

In today's competitive business environment, aligning HR KPIs with organizational goals is essential for achieving long-term success. By ensuring that HR functions like talent acquisition, employee engagement, training, and retention directly contribute to business outcomes such as productivity, profitability, and market competitiveness, HR departments can demonstrate their value as strategic partners. This alignment not only helps drive business performance but also fosters a motivated, engaged, and highly skilled workforce capable of achieving the organization's objectives.

In the next chapter, we will explore how businesses can track, analyze, and adjust their HR KPIs to continuously improve workforce performance and align more effectively with changing organizational goals.

Chapter 3: Key HR KPIs Every Business Should Track

In today's competitive business world, the need for data-driven decision-making is more critical than ever. Human Resources (HR) departments, which have historically been seen as operational support functions, are now integral to the strategy and success of organizations. Tracking and measuring the effectiveness of HR activities through Key Performance Indicators (KPIs) allows businesses to gauge employee satisfaction, productivity, and the overall health of the workforce. By aligning HR KPIs with organizational goals, businesses can drive growth, enhance employee engagement, reduce turnover, and improve operational efficiency.

This chapter will explore the key HR KPIs that every business should track. These KPIs, such as employee turnover rate, time to fill vacancies, employee satisfaction, and training effectiveness, offer a clear picture of how well an organization is managing its human resources. We will dive deep into each KPI, provide examples, explain their significance, and discuss how they contribute to understanding the overall health of the organization.

1. Employee Turnover Rate

One of the most critical HR KPIs that every business should monitor is the **employee turnover rate**. This metric measures the percentage of employees who leave the company during a given period. A high turnover rate can signal deeper issues within the company, such as dissatisfaction with management, company culture, compensation, or work-life balance. Conversely, a low turnover rate indicates that the company is retaining its talent and providing a work environment that encourages employees to stay long-term.

Formula for Employee Turnover Rate:

$$\text{Employee Turnover Rate} = \frac{\text{Number of Employees Who Left During a Period}}{\text{Average Number of Employees During the Same Period}} \times 100$$

Why It's Important:

Tracking the turnover rate helps businesses understand how well they are retaining employees and the reasons for their departure. High turnover rates can be costly for businesses, as recruiting and training new employees can drain resources. Moreover, it often leads to a loss of knowledge and experience, which can impact productivity. Conversely, low turnover indicates employee satisfaction and strong organizational health.

Example:

If a company had 10 employees leave within a year and had an average of 100 employees, the turnover rate would be calculated as follows:

$$\text{Employee Turnover Rate} = \frac{10}{100} \times 100 = 10\%$$

If this turnover rate is deemed too high, the company can take steps to investigate the causes (e.g., poor management, inadequate compensation, lack of career growth opportunities) and address them accordingly.

Actionable Insights:

- A high turnover rate could signal problems with leadership or employee satisfaction.
- Organizations can investigate exit interviews to gather insights and prevent unnecessary departures.
- Offering better employee benefits, career growth opportunities, or improving company culture may reduce turnover.

2. Time to Fill Vacancies

The **time to fill** is another essential KPI for HR departments. It measures how long it takes, from the moment a job opening is posted until an offer is accepted by a candidate. This metric is vital because it reflects the efficiency of the hiring process. A prolonged hiring process can delay project timelines, hinder company performance, and lead to additional costs in terms of temporary staffing or lost productivity.

Formula for Time to Fill Vacancies:

$$\text{Time to Fill} = \frac{\text{Total Days to Fill All Open Positions}}{\text{Total Number of Positions Filled}}$$

Why It's Important:

Tracking time to fill vacancies allows businesses to measure the efficiency of their recruitment efforts and identify areas for improvement. The faster a company can fill vacancies, the less disruption there will be to productivity. If positions remain open for extended periods, it could indicate inefficiencies in the recruitment process or an inability to attract qualified candidates.

Example:

If a company took 30 days to fill 5 job openings, the average time to fill would be calculated as:

$$\text{Time to Fill} = \frac{30}{5} = 6 \text{ days per hire}$$

A low time to fill suggests that the company's recruitment process is efficient. However, if this time increases significantly, HR can reassess its methods and streamline the recruitment process.

Actionable Insights:

- HR should analyze bottlenecks in the hiring process, such as lengthy interview stages or slow feedback loops, and work to eliminate them.

- Implementing an applicant tracking system (ATS) can improve recruitment efficiency and help shorten the hiring cycle.

- Speeding up the process ensures that high-quality candidates are not lost to competitors.

3. Employee Satisfaction

Employee satisfaction is one of the most crucial indicators of overall organizational health. Satisfied employees are more likely to stay with the company, perform well, and contribute to a positive workplace culture. On the other hand, dissatisfied employees can lead to higher turnover, lower productivity, and a negative work environment.

Why It's Important:

Employee satisfaction surveys, often conducted through annual or quarterly surveys, provide valuable insights into the factors that drive employee happiness and engagement. Companies that track employee satisfaction can address concerns early, creating an environment where employees feel heard, valued, and motivated.

Examples of Employee Satisfaction KPIs:

- **Employee Engagement Score:** A score based on how connected employees feel to the company's mission, values, and goals.

- **Job Satisfaction Rating:** A rating given by employees based on their overall happiness with their job responsibilities, work environment, and company culture.

- **Management Satisfaction:** A rating based on employees' satisfaction with leadership and their relationship with direct managers.

Actionable Insights:

- HR can use employee satisfaction data to address specific areas of concern, such as poor management practices, lack of recognition, or insufficient professional development opportunities.
- Regular feedback and open communication channels (e.g., surveys, town halls) help identify and resolve employee issues before they lead to disengagement or turnover.
- Employee satisfaction directly impacts retention, so it is essential to invest in programs that promote a positive work environment.

4. Training Effectiveness

Effective training is critical for developing employees' skills and ensuring that they can contribute to the organization's success. **Training effectiveness** measures how well training programs improve employees' skills and knowledge, ultimately leading to better performance and organizational outcomes. Measuring training effectiveness helps HR determine the return on investment (ROI) for training initiatives and whether employees are gaining the skills necessary to perform their jobs at a high level.

Formula for Training Effectiveness:

$$\text{Training Effectiveness} = \frac{\text{Post-Training Performance Improvement}}{\text{Pre-Training Performance}} \times 100$$

Why It's Important:

Training is an investment, and it's essential to assess whether the resources spent on training are paying off. A lack of measurable improvements in employee performance post-training may indicate that the training is ineffective or not aligned with business goals. Effective training contributes directly to employee productivity, job satisfaction, and retention.

Example:

If employees show a 20% increase in performance after completing a training program (based on performance reviews or KPIs), the training effectiveness can be calculated as:

$$\text{Training Effectiveness} = \frac{20}{10} \times 100 = 200\%$$

This indicates that the training was highly effective in improving employee performance.

Actionable Insights:

- HR should regularly evaluate the effectiveness of training programs through surveys, performance assessments, and feedback from employees and managers.
- If training effectiveness is low, HR should reassess the content, delivery methods, and relevancy of the programs.
- A focus on training that aligns with organizational goals ensures that employees are well-equipped to meet business objectives.

5. Absenteeism Rate

The **absenteeism rate** is another essential KPI that provides insights into employee engagement and overall workplace morale. Frequent absenteeism can be a sign of disengagement, health issues, or workplace dissatisfaction. On the other hand, low absenteeism rates suggest that employees are happy, motivated, and productive.

Formula for Absenteeism Rate:

$$\text{Absenteeism Rate} = \frac{\text{Total Number of Absence Days}}{\text{Total Number of Workdays}} \times 100$$

Why It's Important:

Tracking absenteeism helps HR understand whether employees are taking excessive time off. This information can be used to identify trends, such as an increase in absenteeism in particular departments, or among certain demographics of employees. Additionally, high absenteeism can impact productivity and morale in the workplace, potentially creating a cycle of underperformance.

Example:

If employees took 100 absentee days in a year, and there were 1,000 total workdays, the absenteeism rate would be:

$$\text{Absenteeism Rate} = \frac{100}{1000} \times 100 = 10\%$$

A high absenteeism rate indicates that HR should investigate the root causes, such as poor work conditions, burnout, or inadequate employee support programs.

Actionable Insights:

- HR should work to understand the root causes of absenteeism, including employee dissatisfaction or health-related issues.
- Implementing wellness programs and offering flexible work options can help reduce absenteeism.
- Monitoring absenteeism helps identify problems early, preventing disruptions in work output.

6. Diversity and Inclusion (D&I) Metrics

Tracking diversity and inclusion is crucial for creating a work environment that attracts and retains a diverse talent pool. D&I metrics measure how well an organization is doing in fostering a culture of inclusivity and ensuring equal opportunities for all employees, regardless of gender, race, or background.

Formula for Diversity Rate:

$$\text{Diversity Rate} = \frac{\text{Number of Employees from Diverse Backgrounds}}{\text{Total Number of Employees}} \times 100$$

Why It's Important:

Diversity and inclusion contribute to a richer work environment, where different perspectives are valued. A focus on diversity helps companies tap into a wide range of ideas and fosters creativity and innovation. Moreover, inclusive workplaces often have higher employee satisfaction and retention rates.

Example:

If an organization has 40 employees from diverse backgrounds out of a total of 100 employees, the diversity rate would be:

$$\text{Diversity Rate} = \frac{40}{100} \times 100 = 40\%$$

This indicates that the company has a relatively high level of diversity, which is a positive outcome.

Actionable Insights:

- HR should set clear diversity and inclusion goals, regularly measure progress, and adjust hiring and retention strategies to ensure diversity in the workforce.

- Employee training and awareness programs on unconscious bias and inclusion are essential to creating a truly inclusive workplace.

- Measuring diversity and inclusion helps organizations stay accountable to their D&I goals, fostering an inclusive culture that benefits all employees.

Conclusion

The HR KPIs discussed in this chapter—employee turnover rate, time to fill vacancies, employee satisfaction, training effectiveness, absenteeism rate, and diversity rate—are essential tools for understanding the health of an organization. By regularly monitoring these metrics, businesses can identify areas of improvement, make informed decisions, and ultimately build a strong and sustainable workforce. Each of these KPIs plays a vital role in shaping an organization's culture, performance, and long-term success. When tracked effectively, HR KPIs not only contribute to the well-being of employees but also ensure the achievement of broader organizational goals.

Chapter 4: Measuring Employee Engagement and Satisfaction

Employee engagement and satisfaction are two of the most important factors that contribute to a company's success. They have a profound impact on productivity, retention rates, and the overall health of an organization. In today's competitive business landscape, companies are increasingly recognizing that employees are their most valuable asset, and their engagement and satisfaction play a central role in achieving organizational goals. As a result, measuring and tracking these metrics through specific Key Performance Indicators (KPIs) provides businesses with a clearer understanding of their workforce's morale, motivation, and overall well-being.

This chapter will delve deeply into the concepts of employee engagement and satisfaction, explaining their significance and how they directly influence business outcomes. It will explore various KPIs used to assess engagement and satisfaction, including the **Employee Net Promoter Score (eNPS), Employee Satisfaction Score (ESS)**, and **Employee Engagement Surveys**. Additionally, we will discuss the relationship between employee well-being and organizational success, offering actionable insights for organizations looking to improve engagement and satisfaction levels.

The Importance of Employee Engagement and Satisfaction

Before diving into the specific KPIs used to measure engagement and satisfaction, it's essential to understand why these factors are so critical to an organization's overall health.

Employee Engagement

Employee engagement refers to the emotional commitment that employees have towards their work and the organization. Engaged employees are not just "satisfied" with their jobs—they are passionate, invested, and motivated to go above and beyond their regular responsibilities. They take ownership of their work and contribute actively to the success of the organization. In contrast, disengaged employees are often uninspired, disinterested, and lack the motivation to perform at their best.

The benefits of high employee engagement are well-documented:

- **Increased Productivity**: Engaged employees tend to be more productive, as they are deeply committed to delivering high-quality work.
- **Lower Turnover**: Engagement fosters a sense of loyalty to the organization, which reduces employee

turnover and the associated costs of hiring and training new staff.

- **Improved Customer Satisfaction**: Engaged employees are more likely to provide excellent service to customers, leading to higher customer satisfaction levels and greater customer retention.

- **Enhanced Innovation**: When employees are fully engaged, they are more likely to contribute new ideas and creative solutions to the business.

Employee Satisfaction

Employee satisfaction, on the other hand, refers to how content employees are with various aspects of their job, such as compensation, benefits, work-life balance, career growth opportunities, and the work environment. While satisfaction is an important aspect of overall employee well-being, it does not necessarily indicate the same level of commitment or emotional investment as engagement does.

However, employee satisfaction remains an essential KPI for measuring organizational health because:

- **Job Retention**: Satisfied employees are less likely to leave the organization, which directly impacts turnover rates.

- **Workplace Harmony**: When employees are satisfied, they are more likely to have positive relationships with their colleagues, which contributes to a harmonious work environment.

- **Healthier Work Culture**: Employee satisfaction often correlates with a positive work culture, which encourages collaboration, innovation, and creativity.

- **Reduced Absenteeism**: Satisfied employees are less likely to take frequent sick days or extended leaves, reducing absenteeism rates and maintaining productivity levels.

In short, while employee engagement is a deeper emotional commitment, employee satisfaction serves as an important foundation that enables engagement to thrive. Both are interrelated and equally important for business success.

Key Performance Indicators (KPIs) for Measuring Employee Engagement and Satisfaction

Now that we have established the importance of employee engagement and satisfaction, let's explore some of the most common KPIs used to measure these factors. These KPIs provide valuable data that can help organizations track their progress, identify areas of improvement, and implement targeted strategies for boosting employee engagement and satisfaction.

1. Employee Net Promoter Score (eNPS)

The **Employee Net Promoter Score (eNPS)** is one of the most popular and effective KPIs for measuring employee engagement. Adapted from the Net Promoter Score (NPS), which is used to measure customer loyalty, eNPS gauges how likely employees are to recommend their workplace to others. This score is a direct indicator of how engaged and satisfied employees feel with their employer.

How It Works:

The eNPS survey asks employees a simple question:

"On a scale of 0 to 10, how likely are you to recommend this organization as a place to work?"

Employees respond with a number between 0 and 10, with the following classifications:

- **Promoters (score 9-10):** Employees who are highly engaged, satisfied, and likely to speak positively about the organization.
- **Passives (score 7-8):** Employees who are somewhat satisfied but not as enthusiastic about the company as promoters.
- **Detractors (score 0-6):** Employees who are disengaged, dissatisfied, and unlikely to recommend the organization.

Formula for eNPS:

$$eNPS = \%Promoters - \%Detractors$$

For example, if 70% of employees are promoters and 10% are detractors, the eNPS would be:

$$eNPS = 70\% - 10\% = 60$$

Why It's Important:

The eNPS provides a simple, quantifiable way to assess employee loyalty, engagement, and satisfaction. A high eNPS indicates a strong, engaged workforce, while a low eNPS signals that the organization may have issues with employee morale, work culture, or leadership.

Organizations can track eNPS over time to identify trends and measure the impact of changes in company policies, benefits, or leadership practices. Regular feedback through eNPS helps organizations take proactive steps to address disengagement before it becomes a bigger problem.

2. Employee Satisfaction Score (ESS)

The **Employee Satisfaction Score (ESS)** is a straightforward KPI that measures how satisfied employees are with various aspects of their job, including compensation, work-life balance, job role, career development opportunities, and company culture. It is typically gathered through surveys and questionnaires that ask employees to rate their satisfaction on a scale from 1 to 5 or 1 to 10.

Why It's Important:

The ESS is essential because it provides a snapshot of employee contentment with their job. High satisfaction levels are often indicative of a positive work environment, effective management, and competitive compensation. Conversely, low satisfaction scores can highlight areas of dissatisfaction that need to be addressed, such as low pay, poor work-life balance, or a lack of growth opportunities.

Example:

A simple ESS survey may include questions like:

- *"How satisfied are you with your compensation?"*
- *"How satisfied are you with your work-life balance?"*

- *"How satisfied are you with your career growth opportunities?"*

The average score across all these questions gives an overall satisfaction score.

Actionable Insights:

By tracking ESS scores over time, organizations can identify trends in satisfaction and pinpoint areas where improvements are needed. For example, if employees report low satisfaction with career development opportunities, HR can introduce mentorship programs or additional training to help employees advance within the company.

3. Employee Engagement Surveys

Employee engagement surveys are comprehensive tools used to measure a wide range of factors that contribute to employee engagement. These surveys typically ask employees a series of questions about their job satisfaction, motivation, relationship with management, company culture, and work environment.

Some common questions in an employee engagement survey may include:

- *"Do you feel that your work is appreciated?"*
- *"Do you believe your work contributes to the success of the company?"*
- *"Do you have opportunities for growth and advancement?"*
- *"Do you trust the leadership of this organization?"*

Why It's Important:

Employee engagement surveys help organizations understand the root causes of disengagement and dissatisfaction. They provide deeper insights into specific areas that affect employee motivation, such as leadership, team dynamics, or organizational culture. These surveys often serve as a diagnostic tool to identify problems and create targeted solutions for improving engagement.

Actionable Insights:

Analyzing the responses to engagement surveys allows HR departments to implement effective strategies to increase engagement. For example, if employees report low trust in leadership, management training, transparency in communication, and leadership development programs may be necessary.

4. Retention Rate

While **retention rate** is a more general KPI that measures how well an organization retains its employees, it is also a key indicator of employee engagement and satisfaction. High retention rates typically correlate with high levels of employee satisfaction and engagement, while high turnover can indicate underlying issues with engagement or satisfaction.

Formula for Retention Rate:

$$\text{Retention Rate} = \frac{\text{Number of Employees at End of Period}}{\text{Number of Employees at Start of Period}} \times 100$$

For example, if a company started the year with 100 employees and ended with 90, the retention rate would be:

$$\text{Retention Rate} = \frac{90}{100} \times 100 = 90\%$$

Why It's Important:

A high retention rate indicates that employees are satisfied, engaged, and committed to the company. On the other hand, low retention can be a sign of dissatisfaction, disengagement, or poor work culture, prompting HR to investigate the reasons for turnover and take corrective actions.

The Relationship Between Engagement, Satisfaction, and Organizational Success

Understanding the connection between employee engagement, satisfaction, and organizational success is essential for any business. When employees are engaged and satisfied, they are more likely to be productive, innovative, and loyal to the company. This, in turn, contributes to the company's overall success by improving profitability, customer satisfaction, and operational efficiency.

For example, a study by Gallup found that organizations with highly engaged employees experience 21% higher profitability, 17% higher productivity, and 10% higher customer satisfaction compared to organizations with disengaged employees. Similarly, companies with high employee satisfaction tend to have lower turnover rates, which reduces recruitment and training costs.

Conclusion

Employee engagement and satisfaction are not just "nice-to-haves" for businesses—they are critical to the long-term health and success of an organization. By measuring and tracking key KPIs such as the Employee Net Promoter Score (eNPS), Employee Satisfaction Score (ESS), and retention rates, businesses can gain valuable insights into their workforce's morale, motivation, and overall well-being. These insights allow organizations to make data-driven decisions that improve employee engagement, satisfaction, and, ultimately, business performance. As the world of work continues to evolve, understanding and improving these metrics will remain a vital part of maintaining a thriving and successful organization.

Chapter 5: Enhancing Recruitment and Retention through HR KPIs

Recruitment and retention are two of the most critical aspects of human resources management. A company's ability to attract and retain top talent directly influences its growth, productivity, and competitive edge. As such, Human Resources (HR) professionals rely on various Key Performance Indicators (KPIs) to track and measure the effectiveness of recruitment strategies and retention efforts. These KPIs help organizations identify strengths and weaknesses in their hiring processes, optimize recruitment strategies, reduce hiring costs, and ultimately improve retention rates. In this chapter, we will explore how tracking HR KPIs related to recruitment and retention can lead to better decision-making and enhanced organizational performance.

The Importance of Recruitment and Retention

Before delving into the specifics of recruitment and retention KPIs, it is important to understand why these two elements are so critical to the success of any business.

Recruitment: The Foundation of Organizational Success

Recruitment is the process of attracting, selecting, and hiring the best candidates for open positions within an organization. The quality of the recruitment process has a direct impact on the organization's performance, as the right hire can bring valuable skills, expertise, and fresh perspectives. However, poor recruitment practices can result in high turnover, decreased productivity, and even damage to the company's reputation.

A strong recruitment strategy is essential for ensuring that the organization attracts top talent and fills roles with individuals who fit the company culture, contribute to the organizational goals, and drive innovation.

Retention: The Key to Sustaining a High-Performing Workforce

While recruitment is about bringing new talent into the organization, retention focuses on keeping that talent long-term. Employee retention is the ability of an organization to retain its employees and prevent them from leaving the company. High employee turnover is costly, not only because of the financial burden of recruitment and onboarding but also due to the loss of experience, knowledge, and continuity within the workforce.

Retention is closely linked to employee satisfaction, engagement, career development, compensation, and work-life balance. When employees are happy with their roles, feel valued, and have opportunities for growth, they are more likely to stay with the company and continue contributing to its success.

In this chapter, we will examine several KPIs that are essential for improving recruitment and retention, as well as the benefits they provide in terms of strategic alignment, efficiency, and overall organizational health.

Key Recruitment KPIs

Effective recruitment strategies are grounded in data-driven insights, and KPIs play a crucial role in measuring the success of these strategies. Tracking and analyzing recruitment KPIs helps HR teams understand how well they are sourcing, attracting, and hiring talent. Below, we will look at some of the most important recruitment KPIs.

1. Time to Hire

Time to hire is one of the most commonly used recruitment KPIs. It measures the amount of time it takes to fill an open position, from the moment a job requisition is approved to the time the candidate officially accepts the job offer. This metric is a critical indicator of the efficiency of the recruitment process and can provide insights into bottlenecks or delays that may be slowing down the hiring process.

Formula for Time to Hire:

$$\text{Time to Hire} = \frac{\text{Total Number of Days to Fill a Position}}{\text{Number of Positions Filled}}$$

$$\text{Time to Hire} = \frac{\text{Total Number of Days to Fill a Position}}{\text{Number of Positions Filled}}$$

Why It's Important:

- **Efficiency**: A shorter time to hire means that the recruitment process is efficient, and the organization can fill positions quickly to maintain productivity.

- **Candidate Experience**: Long hiring processes can frustrate candidates and lead to a negative experience. A quicker process reflects well on the company's ability to make decisions and respect candidates' time.

- **Cost Implications**: A prolonged time to hire can increase costs associated with unfilled positions, such as overtime pay for existing employees or a decrease in productivity due to understaffing.

To optimize time to hire, HR teams should regularly evaluate their recruitment process to identify bottlenecks, streamline workflows, and ensure quick decision-making.

2. Cost Per Hire

Cost per hire is a KPI that measures the total cost of hiring a new employee, including advertising, recruitment agency fees, interview costs, onboarding expenses, and any other associated costs. This KPI helps HR teams understand how much the organization is spending to acquire talent and can highlight areas where recruitment costs can be optimized.

Formula for Cost Per Hire:

$$\text{Cost Per Hire} = \frac{\text{Total Recruiting Costs}}{\text{Number of Hires}}$$

For example, if the total recruiting costs for the quarter were $100,000 and the company made 20 hires, the cost per hire would be:

$$\text{Cost Per Hire} = \frac{100,000}{20} = 5,000$$

Why It's Important:

- **Budget Optimization**: By tracking cost per hire, HR teams can identify areas where spending is higher than necessary and adjust their strategies accordingly. This could involve optimizing advertising platforms, reducing agency fees, or automating parts of the recruitment process to reduce costs.

- **Resource Allocation**: If a particular recruitment channel is found to be more cost-effective than others, resources can be reallocated to prioritize that channel.

It is essential to balance cost per hire with the quality of candidates hired. While it's important to keep recruitment costs low, hiring the right talent at the right price is the ultimate goal.

3. Offer Acceptance Rate

The **offer acceptance rate** measures the percentage of job offers accepted by candidates. This KPI is vital for assessing the effectiveness of the company's recruitment efforts, including how competitive the company's compensation package is and how attractive the company is as an employer.

Formula for Offer Acceptance Rate:

$$\text{Offer Acceptance Rate} = \frac{\text{Accepted Offers}}{\text{Total Job Offers}} \times 100$$

For example, if the company made 50 job offers and 40 of them were accepted, the offer acceptance rate would be:

$$\text{Offer Acceptance Rate} = \frac{40}{50} \times 100 = 80\%$$

Why It's Important:

- **Attractiveness of the Offer**: A low offer acceptance rate could indicate that the company's compensation package or benefits are not competitive enough, or that candidates are receiving better offers elsewhere.

- **Employer Branding**: If candidates consistently decline job offers, it may suggest issues with the company's employer brand. Improving employer branding, company culture, and the candidate experience can improve this rate.

A high offer acceptance rate indicates that candidates are interested in working for the company, which means that the organization's recruitment strategy is appealing and effective.

Key Retention KPIs

While recruitment KPIs focus on attracting and hiring talent, retention KPIs measure the organization's ability to keep employees and minimize turnover. A high turnover rate can be costly, as it leads to recruitment and training expenses, loss of productivity, and potential disruption to team dynamics. Below, we will discuss some of the most important retention-related KPIs.

1. Employee Turnover Rate

The **employee turnover rate** is a metric that calculates the percentage of employees who leave the company over a specific period, typically annually. This KPI helps organizations understand how well they are retaining employees and can indicate potential issues with job satisfaction, management, or company culture.

Formula for Employee Turnover Rate:

$$\text{Turnover Rate} = \frac{\text{Number of Employees Who Left}}{\text{Average Number of Employees}} \times 100$$

For example, if 15 employees left during the year and the average number of employees was 150, the turnover rate would be:

$$\text{Turnover Rate} = \frac{15}{150} \times 100 = 10\%$$

Why It's Important:

- **Retention Issues**: A high turnover rate may signal problems such as poor management, lack of growth opportunities, or employee dissatisfaction.

- **Cost of Turnover**: High turnover rates are costly because they require additional resources to recruit, hire, and train new employees. By identifying the causes of turnover, HR can implement strategies to improve retention and reduce these costs.

Reducing turnover requires identifying the root causes of employee dissatisfaction and addressing them through improved management practices, employee development programs, and competitive compensation.

2. Employee Retention Rate

While turnover rate focuses on employees leaving the organization, the **employee retention rate** measures the percentage of employees who stay with the organization over a given period. High retention rates suggest that employees are satisfied and engaged, while low retention rates indicate potential issues with morale or job satisfaction.

Formula for Employee Retention Rate:

$$\text{Retention Rate} = \frac{\text{Number of Employees at End of Period} - \text{Number of Employees Who Left}}{\text{Number of Employees at Start of Period}} \times 100$$

For example, if a company started the year with 100 employees and had 10 employees leave, the retention rate would be:

$$\text{Retention Rate} = \frac{100 - 10}{100} \times 100 = 90\%$$

Why It's Important:

- **Employee Satisfaction**: A high retention rate typically indicates that employees are satisfied with their work, the company culture, and the benefits offered.
- **Cost Savings**: Retaining employees helps save costs related to recruiting, onboarding, and training new hires. It also ensures that the company maintains experienced, knowledgeable employees.

Improving employee retention often involves fostering a positive work culture, offering opportunities for growth and development, and ensuring competitive compensation packages.

Conclusion: Leveraging Recruitment and Retention KPIs

Recruitment and retention are two of the most crucial aspects of human resources management, and KPIs provide the data needed to optimize these processes. By tracking KPIs such as time to hire, cost per hire, offer acceptance rate, turnover rate, and retention rate, HR teams can make data-driven decisions that lead to more efficient hiring processes, reduced turnover, and a more satisfied, engaged workforce.

Unlocking Business Success

Organizations that successfully track and leverage these KPIs can better align their recruitment and retention strategies with their overall business goals, ensuring that they attract and keep the right talent to drive growth, productivity, and success. As businesses continue to evolve and face new challenges, having robust recruitment and retention strategies in place will remain essential for maintaining a healthy and high-performing workforce.

Chapter 6: Assessing Learning and Development through KPIs

In an ever-evolving business landscape, continuous learning and development (L&D) have become essential for maintaining a competitive edge. The capacity for an organization to grow its employees' skills and competencies directly affects its long-term business health, productivity, and success. Effective learning and development programs lead to an empowered, skilled workforce that is equipped to meet the demands of the market and adapt to change.

One of the most effective ways to assess the effectiveness of these programs and initiatives is through Key Performance Indicators (KPIs). These KPIs help HR professionals and business leaders measure whether training programs are successful, identify skill gaps, and determine areas for improvement. In this chapter, we will explore how KPIs related to training effectiveness, employee development, and learning opportunities impact overall employee performance, business growth, and organizational success.

The Importance of Learning and Development in Business Health

Before delving into the specific KPIs used to assess learning and development (L&D) initiatives, it is important to first understand why L&D is so critical for a company's overall health.

1. Adapting to Industry Changes

Industries are changing at an unprecedented rate, with technology, regulations, and market trends evolving quickly. In order to remain competitive, businesses must ensure that their employees are continuously updated with the latest knowledge, tools, and techniques in their respective fields. Training and development programs equip employees with the skills and capabilities needed to respond to new challenges and emerging opportunities.

2. Employee Performance and Productivity

Effective L&D programs enhance employee performance by equipping staff with the necessary skills to succeed in their roles. By investing in continuous development, organizations can foster a more skilled and motivated workforce. This leads to improved performance, higher productivity, and ultimately, greater business outcomes. L&D programs contribute to creating high-performing teams that are capable of delivering on business goals and driving results.

3. Employee Engagement and Retention

Organizations that prioritize employee learning and development foster a culture of growth and opportunity. When employees have access to training and career development resources, they are more likely to feel engaged in their work and committed to the company. This, in turn, improves retention rates, as employees who feel valued and supported are less likely to seek employment elsewhere. Providing opportunities for personal and professional growth is a key factor in ensuring long-term retention and job satisfaction.

4. Future Leadership Development

In addition to enhancing the skills of current employees, L&D programs also play a critical role in developing future leaders. Organizations that invest in leadership training and succession planning are better equipped to cultivate talent from within and ensure that they have a strong pipeline of leaders ready to take on key roles in the future. This investment in leadership development creates organizational continuity, stability, and success over the long term.

With these benefits in mind, it is clear that learning and development initiatives are not only crucial for individual employees but also for the overall success and growth of a business. The next step is to evaluate how KPIs can help track the success and impact of these programs.

The Role of KPIs in Learning and Development

KPIs are essential for evaluating the effectiveness of training programs and ensuring that investments in learning and development align with business objectives. KPIs related to L&D provide data-driven insights into how well employees are developing new skills, how effectively training programs are implemented, and whether the programs are having a positive impact on business performance.

Using KPIs to measure L&D success helps organizations:

1. **Identify Gaps**: Understand where employees or teams are lacking in skills and knowledge and prioritize areas for further development.
2. **Measure Effectiveness**: Assess whether training programs are achieving their intended outcomes and improving employee performance.
3. **Align with Business Goals**: Ensure that L&D initiatives are aligned with the organization's broader goals, strategies, and objectives.
4. **Optimize Training Investments**: Optimize training resources and investments by evaluating the ROI of learning and development programs.

Below, we will explore some of the most important L&D KPIs that can help organizations measure the effectiveness of their training and development initiatives.

Key Learning and Development KPIs

1. Training Completion Rate

The **training completion rate** measures the percentage of employees who successfully complete a given training program. A high training completion rate indicates that employees are engaged in the learning process and that the program is accessible and effective. On the other hand, a low completion rate might signal that the training is too lengthy, complicated, or not compelling enough to maintain employee interest.

Formula for Training Completion Rate:

$$\text{Training Completion Rate} = \frac{\text{Number of Employees Who Completed Training}}{\text{Number of Employees Enrolled in Training}} \times 100$$

For example, if 100 employees were enrolled in a training program and 80 completed it, the completion rate would be:

$$\text{Training Completion Rate} = \frac{80}{100} \times 100 = 80\%$$

Why It's Important:

- **Engagement and Participation**: A higher completion rate reflects good employee engagement and participation. It suggests that employees value the training and are committed to completing it.
- **Training Design**: If the completion rate is low, it may indicate that the training content or format needs to be improved to better engage employees.

Organizations can improve this KPI by making training more accessible, breaking it into smaller modules, and ensuring that employees see the value in completing the program.

2. Training Effectiveness

Training effectiveness measures how well a training program enhances employee knowledge, skills, and performance. This KPI typically involves post-training assessments, surveys, and feedback to determine whether employees have gained the necessary competencies from the training program.

Formula for Training Effectiveness:

$$\text{Training Effectiveness} = \frac{\text{Post-Training Score} - \text{Pre-Training Score}}{\text{Pre-Training Score}} \times 100$$

For example, if an employee's test score increased from 60% to 80% after completing the training, the training effectiveness would be:

$$\text{Training Effectiveness} = \frac{80 - 60}{60} \times 100 = 33.33\%$$

Why It's Important:

- **Skills Development**: This KPI shows how much employees have learned and whether the training content is aligned with their developmental needs.

- **Return on Investment (ROI)**: Measuring training effectiveness allows HR professionals and leaders to assess whether the resources spent on training are producing measurable improvements in employee performance.

This KPI can be further refined by breaking down the effectiveness based on different training modules or skill areas to ensure that the training program is comprehensive and impactful.

3. Employee Satisfaction with Training Programs

Employee satisfaction with training programs is another critical KPI. This metric gauges how satisfied employees are with the quality, content, delivery, and overall experience of the training programs. It can be measured through surveys or feedback forms that assess employees' views on the training's relevance, clarity, and utility.

Formula for Employee Satisfaction with Training Programs:

$$\text{Employee Satisfaction} = \frac{\text{Total Satisfaction Score}}{\text{Total Number of Respondents}} \times 100$$

For example, if the total satisfaction score from 50 employees is 400 (on a scale of 1-10), the satisfaction score would be:

$$\text{Employee Satisfaction} = \frac{400}{50} = 8 \text{ (out of 10)}$$

Why It's Important:

- **Engagement and Motivation**: Employee satisfaction is a direct indicator of how motivated employees are to apply what they've learned. A highly satisfied employee is more likely to implement new knowledge and share their insights with others.
- **Continuous Improvement**: Employee feedback helps improve training programs and ensure that they

remain relevant and engaging. By listening to employees' preferences and concerns, HR teams can refine training strategies.

Organizations should aim for high satisfaction scores, as satisfied employees are more likely to retain the knowledge gained and apply it to their work.

4. Knowledge Retention Rate

Knowledge retention refers to the ability of employees to retain the knowledge and skills they learned in a training program over time. This KPI can be measured by conducting follow-up assessments after a period of time has passed since the training session. High retention rates indicate that the training program was impactful and that employees are able to transfer their learning to their work effectively.

Formula for Knowledge Retention Rate:

$$\text{Knowledge Retention Rate} = \frac{\text{Post-Training Assessment Score}}{\text{Initial Training Assessment Score}} \times 100$$

For example, if an employee scored 75% in the initial assessment and 70% in a follow-up assessment three months later, the knowledge retention rate would be:

$$\text{Knowledge Retention Rate} = \frac{70}{75} \times 100 = 93.33\%$$

Why It's Important:

- **Long-Term Impact**: Knowledge retention measures the long-term impact of training programs on employee performance. Effective training should result in lasting improvements, not just short-term knowledge gains.

- **Program Effectiveness**: Low retention rates may indicate that the training program did not effectively solidify the learning, requiring changes to the content or delivery methods.

To improve knowledge retention, organizations should implement strategies such as spaced learning, refresher courses, and on-the-job application of skills.

5. Career Development and Promotion Rate

The **career development and promotion rate** measures how effectively the organization is helping employees progress in their careers. This KPI tracks the number of employees who are promoted or given new responsibilities after completing training programs.

Formula for Career Development and Promotion Rate:

$$\text{Career Development Rate} = \frac{\text{Number of Employees Promoted}}{\text{Total Number of Employees Who Completed Training}} \times 100$$

Why It's Important:

- **Career Growth:** This KPI demonstrates whether the organization is successfully developing employees for higher-level roles. A higher promotion rate is an indication of a successful training program that prepares employees for increased responsibility.

- **Employee Retention:** Career development opportunities are a key factor in employee retention. Employees who see a clear pathway for advancement within the organization are more likely to stay and contribute to long-term success.

By tracking career development and promotion rates, businesses can ensure they are providing meaningful growth opportunities for employees, helping them retain top talent and build leadership pipelines.

Conclusion

In today's rapidly changing business environment, learning and development are essential for maintaining a competitive edge, improving employee performance, and fostering long-term business success. KPIs related to training effectiveness, employee development, and learning opportunities offer valuable insights into the impact of training programs, enabling organizations to make data-driven decisions that align with their strategic goals.

By leveraging these KPIs, businesses can assess the effectiveness of their L&D initiatives, identify areas for improvement, and ensure that their workforce is equipped with the skills and knowledge necessary to thrive in an ever-evolving market. Whether it's through improving training completion rates, assessing employee satisfaction, or measuring knowledge retention, these KPIs provide a comprehensive view of an organization's learning and development landscape, ultimately driving continuous improvement and success.

Chapter 7: Understanding the Impact of Compensation and Benefits KPIs

In today's competitive business environment, organizations must not only focus on the strategic direction of their business but also on attracting, retaining, and motivating talent. One of the most significant ways companies do this is through their compensation and benefits packages. A well-designed compensation and benefits structure is a critical tool for attracting and retaining top talent, ensuring employee satisfaction, and maintaining a competitive edge in the marketplace.

While offering a competitive salary is crucial, benefits such as health insurance, retirement plans, bonuses, and paid time off play a pivotal role in shaping the overall compensation strategy. To evaluate the effectiveness of these HR strategies, businesses must utilize Key Performance Indicators (KPIs) that provide insight into the competitiveness, satisfaction, and financial sustainability of compensation and benefits packages.

In this chapter, we will explore the impact of compensation and benefits KPIs on an organization's ability to attract and retain employees, the relationship between compensation and business performance, and the importance of measuring the effectiveness of compensation and benefits programs.

The Importance of Compensation and Benefits in Organizational Success

1. Attracting and Retaining Talent

A company's ability to offer competitive compensation and benefits directly impacts its success in attracting top talent. The most qualified candidates are highly likely to consider compensation packages when evaluating job offers. In addition to salary, benefits packages are often viewed as an indicator of a company's commitment to employee well-being and job satisfaction. Offering a well-rounded package that includes healthcare, retirement benefits, paid time off, and other perks enhances the overall value proposition of an organization, making it more attractive to high-quality candidates.

Similarly, compensation and benefits are key to employee retention. Employees who feel that they are fairly compensated for their work are more likely to stay with the organization. If compensation packages are not competitive, employees may be enticed by better offers from other companies, leading to higher turnover rates. Retention becomes even more crucial in today's job market, where attracting top talent can be challenging.

2. Motivating Employees to Perform at Their Best

Effective compensation and benefits strategies also contribute to employee motivation and job satisfaction. When employees feel that their efforts are adequately rewarded, they are more likely to be motivated to perform well. A competitive salary, along with benefits such as performance bonuses or profit-sharing, provides employees with tangible incentives to work harder and exceed expectations.

Additionally, benefits like wellness programs, learning and development opportunities, and paid time off contribute to overall employee satisfaction, ensuring that employees remain engaged and committed to their roles. These factors create a positive work culture that fosters both individual and organizational growth.

3. Supporting Business Sustainability

Compensation and benefits strategies are not just about employee satisfaction—they also play a crucial role in the financial health and sustainability of the organization. While offering attractive compensation packages is important, businesses must also ensure that they are managing these expenses in a way that does not jeopardize profitability or financial stability. This balance can be achieved by tracking and measuring compensation and benefits KPIs, which help HR professionals and business leaders make data-driven decisions that align with both employee needs and business goals.

By focusing on the effectiveness of their compensation and benefits strategies, companies can optimize their budgets and make informed decisions about where to allocate resources for maximum impact.

Key Compensation and Benefits KPIs

Compensation and benefits KPIs are metrics used to assess the effectiveness, competitiveness, and sustainability of compensation and benefits packages. These KPIs provide insight into how well compensation strategies align with business objectives, employee satisfaction, and industry standards. Below, we will discuss the most important KPIs that businesses should track to measure the success of their compensation and benefits programs.

1. Compensation Competitiveness Ratio

The **compensation competitiveness ratio** measures how a company's salary structure compares to the market average for similar positions in the same industry and geographic area. This KPI helps organizations assess whether their compensation offerings are competitive enough to attract and retain top talent.

Formula for Compensation Competitiveness Ratio:

$$\text{Compensation Competitiveness Ratio} = \frac{\text{Average Salary of Employees}}{\text{Market Average Salary for Similar Roles}} \times 100$$

For example, if the average salary for a role in your company is $70,000 and the market average for the same role is $75,000, the compensation competitiveness ratio would be:

$$\text{Compensation Competitiveness Ratio} = \frac{70,000}{75,000} \times 100 = 93.33\%$$

Why It's Important:

- **Attraction and Retention**: A ratio lower than 100% indicates that the company may not be offering competitive salaries, which could affect its ability to attract and retain talent.

- **Salary Benchmarking**: Regularly tracking this KPI ensures that the company is aligned with market trends and can adjust compensation to meet industry standards.

- **Budgeting and Planning**: This KPI helps HR teams forecast compensation adjustments and ensure that the organization remains competitive in attracting top-tier talent without exceeding budgetary constraints.

Tracking compensation competitiveness helps HR professionals remain agile in adjusting salary structures as the labor market evolves.

2. Benefits Satisfaction Score

The **benefits satisfaction score** measures employees' satisfaction with the benefits package offered by the organization. This KPI is typically gathered through employee surveys or feedback forms where employees rate their satisfaction with various benefits, such as healthcare, retirement plans, wellness programs, and paid time off.

Formula for Benefits Satisfaction Score:

$$\text{Benefits Satisfaction Score} = \frac{\text{Total Satisfaction Score}}{\text{Number of Employees Responding to the Survey}} \times 100$$

For example, if 50 employees provide satisfaction ratings, and the total score from all responses is 400 (on a scale of 1-10), the benefits satisfaction score would be:

$$\text{Benefits Satisfaction Score} = \frac{400}{50} = 8 \text{ (out of 10)}$$

Why It's Important:

- **Employee Retention**: A high benefits satisfaction score indicates that employees feel their needs are being met in terms of healthcare, retirement, and other benefits, which leads to higher retention.

- **Workplace Culture**: Benefits play a significant role in fostering a positive work culture. Employees who are satisfied with their benefits are more likely to be engaged and committed to their roles.

- **Continuous Improvement**: Gathering feedback on benefits satisfaction helps HR teams identify areas where the benefits package could be improved, ensuring that the company remains competitive in offering attractive perks.

Regularly evaluating employee satisfaction with benefits is essential to maintaining a positive employee experience.

3. Health Insurance Costs per Employee

Health insurance costs per employee is a KPI that measures the cost to the organization for providing healthcare benefits to employees. This metric is important for assessing the financial sustainability of the organization's benefits offering, as healthcare costs can be a significant expenditure for employers.

Formula for Health Insurance Costs per Employee:

$$\text{Health Insurance Costs per Employee} = \frac{\text{Total Annual Health Insurance Costs}}{\text{Total Number of Employees}}$$

For example, if a company spends $500,000 annually on health insurance for 100 employees, the health insurance costs per employee would be:

$$\text{Health Insurance Costs per Employee} = \frac{500,000}{100} = 5,000$$

Why It's Important:

- **Cost Management**: By tracking this KPI, organizations can ensure that their healthcare spending remains manageable and explore options for cost-saving without sacrificing the quality of benefits provided to employees.

- **Budgeting**: It helps HR professionals and business leaders plan for future healthcare costs, ensuring that compensation packages are financially sustainable.

- **Benchmarking**: Comparing health insurance costs per employee with industry standards allows the organization to determine whether it is spending more or less than average on employee healthcare, which can influence decisions about benefit offerings.

While health insurance costs can be a significant financial burden, they are also crucial for ensuring employee well-being, so it's essential to track this KPI regularly.

4. Turnover Rate Due to Compensation and Benefits

The **turnover rate due to compensation and benefits** tracks the percentage of employees who leave the organization specifically because they are dissatisfied with their compensation or benefits packages. This KPI helps HR professionals understand the impact of compensation and benefits on employee retention and provides insight into areas where improvements may be needed.

Formula for Turnover Rate Due to Compensation and Benefits:

$$\text{Turnover Rate Due to Compensation and Benefits} =$$

$$\frac{\text{Number of Employees Who Left Due to Compensation}}{\text{Total Number of Employees}} \times 100$$

For example, if 10 employees leave due to compensation dissatisfaction out of 200 total employees, the turnover rate would be:

$$\text{Turnover Rate Due to Compensation and Benefits} =$$

$$\frac{10}{200} \times 100 = 5\%$$

Why It's Important:

- **Retention Issues**: A high turnover rate due to compensation issues indicates that employees are dissatisfied with their compensation or benefits packages, which may lead to increased recruitment and training costs.

- **Competitive Edge**: Identifying compensation-driven turnover allows organizations to make necessary adjustments to their salary and benefits structures, helping them remain competitive in attracting and retaining talent.

By tracking this KPI, businesses can gain a deeper understanding of how compensation and benefits impact employee retention and take steps to improve their offerings accordingly.

5. Compensation and Benefits Cost as a Percentage of Revenue

The **compensation and benefits cost as a percentage of revenue** measures the proportion of the company's revenue that is spent on employee compensation and benefits. This KPI helps organizations assess whether their compensation strategies are financially sustainable and whether adjustments are necessary to align compensation costs with overall business performance.

Formula for Compensation and Benefits Cost as a Percentage of Revenue:

$$\text{Compensation and Benefits Cost as a Percentage of Revenue} = \frac{\text{Total Compensation and Benefits Costs}}{\text{Total Revenue}} \times 100$$

For example, if the company spends $2 million on compensation and benefits, and its total revenue is $10 million, the KPI would be:

$$\text{Compensation and Benefits Cost as a Percentage of Revenue} = \frac{2,000,000}{10,000,000} \times 100 = 20\%$$

Why It's Important:

- **Financial Sustainability**: This KPI helps businesses evaluate whether they are spending too much on compensation and benefits, which could affect profitability.

- **Strategic Alignment**: Tracking this KPI ensures that compensation and benefits strategies align with the company's financial goals and overall budget.

- **Cost Control**: If the cost of compensation and benefits is too high relative to revenue, businesses can explore ways to optimize these costs, such as revising compensation structures, renegotiating benefit plans, or adjusting other business expenses.

Conclusion

Compensation and benefits are fundamental to an organization's ability to attract, retain, and motivate employees. Tracking KPIs related to compensation and benefits enables HR professionals and business leaders to assess the effectiveness, competitiveness, and sustainability of their compensation strategies.

By leveraging KPIs like compensation competitiveness ratios, benefits satisfaction scores, health insurance costs per employee, turnover rates, and compensation costs as a percentage of revenue, businesses can make informed decisions that not only align with their financial goals but also promote employee satisfaction and retention. In a world where attracting and retaining top talent is crucial to business success, measuring and optimizing compensation and benefits is a strategic priority for any organization.

Chapter 8: Driving Diversity and Inclusion with HR KPIs

A diverse and inclusive workforce is increasingly recognized as a key driver of innovation, employee engagement, and business success. Organizations with strong diversity and inclusion (D&I) initiatives are better equipped to adapt to a globalized market, attract top talent, and foster a culture of collaboration. However, achieving these outcomes requires more than just good intentions; it demands a strategic approach and measurable goals.

This chapter explores how HR professionals can leverage Key Performance Indicators (KPIs) to track progress in creating a more inclusive and balanced workplace culture. By setting clear metrics and analyzing results, organizations can identify gaps, implement targeted strategies, and hold themselves accountable for advancing D&I objectives.

Why Diversity and Inclusion Matter

Before diving into specific KPIs, it is essential to understand why D&I is critical to organizational success. Research consistently shows that diverse teams outperform homogeneous ones in problem-solving, creativity, and decision-making. Inclusion—the practice of ensuring all employees feel valued and empowered—magnifies these benefits by fostering a culture where individuals can thrive.

Benefits of Diversity and Inclusion:

1. **Enhanced Innovation**: Diverse teams bring varied perspectives, leading to more innovative ideas and solutions.

2. **Broader Talent Pool**: Companies prioritizing D&I can attract top talent from underrepresented groups.

3. **Improved Employee Engagement**: Inclusive environments promote higher morale and job satisfaction.

4. **Market Competitiveness**: Diverse organizations are better positioned to understand and meet the needs of a global customer base.

5. **Stronger Employer Brand**: Commitment to D&I boosts reputation and makes the organization more attractive to job seekers.

Despite these advantages, achieving meaningful progress in D&I requires intentional efforts and measurable outcomes. This is where HR KPIs come into play.

Key HR KPIs for Diversity and Inclusion

To effectively drive D&I initiatives, organizations must track specific metrics that provide insights into representation, equity, and inclusion. Below are some of the most impactful KPIs:

1. Workforce Demographics

Workforce demographics measure the representation of various groups within an organization, including gender, race, ethnicity, age, and disability status. This KPI provides a baseline for assessing diversity and identifying underrepresented groups.

How to Measure:

- Percentage of employees by demographic categories.
- Representation in leadership roles versus overall workforce.
- Comparison to industry benchmarks or local population demographics.

Why It Matters:

Workforce demographics highlight disparities and help organizations focus their recruitment and retention efforts on building a more balanced team.

2. Hiring and Promotion Rates

Tracking the diversity of hires and promotions ensures that opportunities are equitably distributed across all groups. This

KPI helps identify potential biases in hiring practices or career advancement processes.

How to Measure:

- Percentage of new hires from underrepresented groups.
- Promotion rates by demographic category.
- Drop-off rates at each stage of the hiring process (e.g., application, interview, offer).

Why It Matters:

Organizations that prioritize equitable hiring and promotion practices are more likely to build diverse leadership pipelines and reduce systemic barriers to advancement.

3. Pay Equity

Pay equity measures whether employees receive fair compensation regardless of their gender, race, ethnicity, or other characteristics. Addressing pay disparities is a critical component of fostering an inclusive workplace.

How to Measure:

- Median salary by demographic category.
- Pay gaps within equivalent roles and levels of experience.
- Ratio of female to male earnings or minority to non-minority earnings.

Why It Matters:

Transparent and equitable pay practices demonstrate a commitment to fairness and build trust among employees.

4. Inclusion Index

An inclusion index gauges employees' perceptions of inclusivity within the workplace. This KPI combines data from employee surveys to measure whether individuals feel valued, respected, and empowered to contribute.

How to Measure:

- Employee responses to inclusion-related survey questions (e.g., "I feel my opinions are valued at work").
- Net Inclusion Score: Percentage of employees who strongly agree with positive inclusion statements.
- Disaggregating results by demographic group to uncover differences in experience.

Why It Matters:

A high inclusion index indicates that D&I efforts are translating into tangible cultural changes.

5. Retention Rates of Underrepresented Groups

Retention rates measure the ability to retain employees from diverse backgrounds over time. High turnover among specific groups may signal issues with workplace inclusion or equity.

How to Measure:

- Percentage of employees from underrepresented groups who leave the organization within a specified period.
- Exit interview analysis to identify reasons for departure.

Why It Matters:

Retention rates reflect the success of D&I initiatives in creating an environment where diverse employees can thrive.

6. Supplier Diversity

Supplier diversity tracks the percentage of organizational spending directed toward businesses owned by underrepresented groups, such as women, minorities, veterans, or people with disabilities.

How to Measure:

- Percentage of procurement budget spent on diverse suppliers.
- Number of certified diverse suppliers engaged.

Why It Matters:

Supplier diversity extends the principles of inclusion beyond the workforce and demonstrates a commitment to supporting underrepresented communities.

7. Training Completion Rates

Diversity and inclusion training programs aim to raise awareness, reduce biases, and equip employees with skills to foster inclusivity. Tracking participation and completion rates provides insights into the organization's commitment to education and change.

How to Measure:

- Percentage of employees who complete mandatory D&I training.
- Post-training survey results to assess knowledge retention and attitude shifts.

Why It Matters:

Training completion rates reflect an organization's efforts to cultivate a culture of continuous learning and improvement in D&I.

8. Employee Resource Group (ERG) Participation

Employee resource groups (ERGs) are voluntary, employee-led groups that foster a sense of community and belonging. Monitoring ERG participation rates can indicate the level of employee engagement with D&I initiatives.

How to Measure:

- Number of active ERGs.
- Percentage of employees involved in ERGs.
- Frequency and impact of ERG events or initiatives.

Why It Matters:

Strong ERG participation demonstrates that employees value opportunities to connect and collaborate on D&I issues.

9. Diversity in Succession Planning

Diversity in succession planning ensures that leadership pipelines include candidates from underrepresented groups. This KPI highlights whether the organization is actively preparing diverse talent for future leadership roles.

How to Measure:

- Percentage of succession candidates from underrepresented groups.
- Demographic diversity of leadership development program participants.

Why It Matters:

Inclusive succession planning ensures that organizations remain diverse at all levels, including the C-suite.

Strategies for Implementing D&I KPIs

While identifying relevant KPIs is essential, success ultimately depends on how these metrics are implemented and acted upon. Below are strategies for effectively integrating D&I KPIs into organizational practices:

1. Set Clear Goals

Define specific, measurable objectives for each KPI. For example, aim to increase the percentage of women in leadership roles by 10% within three years.

2. Collect and Analyze Data

Gather accurate and comprehensive data through employee surveys, HR records, and external benchmarking. Use data analytics tools to uncover trends and identify areas for improvement.

3. Engage Leadership

Secure buy-in from senior leaders by demonstrating how D&I contributes to business outcomes. Encourage leaders to champion initiatives and hold them accountable for progress.

4. Foster Transparency

Communicate D&I goals and progress openly with employees, stakeholders, and the public. Transparency builds trust and reinforces commitment.

5. Act on Insights

Use KPI data to inform decision-making and prioritize actions. For example, if retention rates for minority employees are low, focus on enhancing inclusion efforts and addressing barriers.

Conclusion

Driving diversity and inclusion is not just a moral imperative; it is a business necessity. By leveraging HR KPIs, organizations can move beyond rhetoric to achieve measurable progress.

Unlocking Business Success

These metrics provide a roadmap for identifying gaps, celebrating successes, and continuously improving.

With a strategic approach to D&I KPIs, businesses can create a workplace culture that values every individual, drives innovation, and achieves long-term success.

Chapter 9: The Role of HR KPIs in Business Strategy and Decision-Making

In today's data-driven world, organizations cannot afford to make decisions based on intuition alone. Strategic decision-making requires actionable insights, and HR Key Performance Indicators (KPIs) play a pivotal role in aligning workforce management with overarching business goals. These metrics provide leaders with a clear picture of organizational health, enabling them to make informed decisions about resource allocation, workforce planning, and change management.

This chapter explores how HR KPIs inform business strategy and drive decision-making processes, offering a comprehensive guide to leveraging HR data for long-term success.

The Intersection of HR and Business Strategy

HR is no longer confined to administrative functions; it is a strategic partner in achieving business objectives. Effective use of HR KPIs bridges the gap between workforce management and broader organizational goals by providing data that:

- Highlights workforce strengths and weaknesses.
- Anticipates future challenges and opportunities.
- Aligns employee performance with business outcomes.

When HR professionals understand the strategic implications of KPIs, they can contribute to decisions that impact profitability, competitiveness, and sustainability.

Key HR KPIs That Drive Strategic Decision-Making

While all HR KPIs provide valuable insights, certain metrics are particularly impactful in shaping business strategy. Below are some of the most critical KPIs and their applications:

1. Employee Turnover Rate

Employee turnover rate measures the percentage of employees who leave an organization within a given timeframe. High turnover rates can signal issues with job satisfaction, leadership, or compensation.

Strategic Applications:

- Identifying departments or roles with high turnover to address underlying issues.
- Forecasting recruitment needs and allocating resources accordingly.
- Evaluating the effectiveness of retention strategies.

2. Time to Fill Vacancies

This KPI tracks the average time taken to fill open positions. A lengthy hiring process can result in lost productivity and missed opportunities.

Strategic Applications:

- Streamlining recruitment processes to reduce downtime.
- Identifying bottlenecks in talent acquisition.
- Enhancing employer branding to attract candidates more efficiently.

3. Employee Engagement and Satisfaction

Employee engagement reflects the level of commitment and enthusiasm employees have toward their work, while satisfaction measures their overall happiness within the organization.

Strategic Applications:

- Linking engagement levels to productivity and profitability metrics.
- Designing initiatives to improve morale and reduce absenteeism.
- Strengthening organizational culture to boost retention.

4. Training Effectiveness

This KPI evaluates the impact of learning and development (L&D) programs on employee performance and skills.

Strategic Applications:

- Aligning training programs with business goals.
- Identifying skill gaps and prioritizing development efforts.
- Measuring ROI on L&D investments.

5. Workforce Productivity

Workforce productivity measures output relative to input, offering insights into operational efficiency.

Strategic Applications:

- Identifying inefficiencies and reallocating resources.
- Setting performance benchmarks for teams and individuals.

- Enhancing workflows to boost overall productivity.

6. Diversity and Inclusion Metrics

D&I KPIs track the representation of various demographic groups and the inclusivity of workplace practices.

Strategic Applications:

- Enhancing innovation through diverse perspectives.
- Meeting compliance requirements and improving corporate reputation.
- Building a workforce that reflects customer demographics.

7. Absenteeism Rate

This KPI measures the average number of days employees are absent from work, excluding planned vacations.

Strategic Applications:

- Addressing root causes of absenteeism, such as burnout or health issues.
- Evaluating the effectiveness of wellness programs.
- Forecasting staffing needs to maintain productivity.

8. Cost Per Hire

Cost per hire evaluates the financial investment required to recruit a new employee. It includes advertising, recruitment agency fees, and onboarding expenses.

Strategic Applications:

- Optimizing recruitment budgets by identifying cost-saving opportunities.
- Evaluating the ROI of different hiring channels.
- Balancing cost efficiency with candidate quality.

How HR KPIs Inform Strategic Decisions

The real value of HR KPIs lies in their ability to transform raw data into actionable insights. Here's how organizations can use HR metrics to guide decision-making:

1. Resource Allocation

HR KPIs help identify areas where resources are most needed. For example, high turnover rates in a specific department may justify additional investment in leadership training or team-building initiatives.

2. Organizational Change

Metrics like employee engagement and satisfaction provide a pulse on workforce sentiment, enabling leaders to anticipate resistance to change and tailor communication strategies.

3. Future Workforce Planning

Data on time to fill vacancies and skill gaps informs long-term workforce planning. Organizations can proactively address talent shortages and succession planning.

4. Risk Management

KPIs such as absenteeism rates and compliance metrics highlight potential risks, allowing organizations to mitigate issues before they escalate.

Implementing HR KPIs in Strategic Planning

To maximize the impact of HR KPIs, organizations must integrate these metrics into their strategic planning processes. Below are steps to ensure seamless implementation:

1. Align KPIs with Business Goals

Identify the KPIs most relevant to achieving organizational objectives. For example, a company focused on innovation may prioritize D&I metrics and training effectiveness.

2. Invest in Data Analytics Tools

Leverage technology to collect, analyze, and visualize HR data. Advanced analytics platforms enable real-time monitoring and predictive insights.

3. Engage Stakeholders

Collaborate with leaders across departments to ensure alignment and buy-in. Present HR KPIs as tools for achieving shared goals rather than isolated metrics.

4. Foster a Culture of Accountability

Hold leaders and managers accountable for meeting KPI targets. Incorporate these metrics into performance evaluations and incentive structures.

5. Continuously Evaluate and Adjust

Regularly review KPI performance to ensure they remain aligned with evolving business needs. Adapt strategies based on data-driven insights.

Case Study: Using HR KPIs to Drive Growth

Consider a mid-sized technology company struggling with high turnover among software engineers. By analyzing HR KPIs, the organization identified key issues:

- **High Turnover Rate**: Exit interviews revealed dissatisfaction with career development opportunities.
- **Low Engagement Scores**: Survey data indicated a lack of recognition and growth.
- **Skill Gaps**: Workforce analytics highlighted emerging needs in artificial intelligence and machine learning.

Armed with these insights, the company implemented targeted interventions:

1. **Enhanced Training Programs**: Introduced certifications in AI and machine learning to upskill employees.
2. **Leadership Development**: Launched mentoring programs to improve career advancement pathways.

3. **Recognition Initiatives**: Established monthly awards for outstanding contributions.

Within a year, the company reported:

- A 25% reduction in turnover.
- A 15% increase in engagement scores.
- Improved project delivery times due to enhanced skills.

Conclusion

HR KPIs are more than just numbers; they are powerful tools that shape the future of an organization. By integrating these metrics into strategic decision-making, leaders can drive meaningful change, optimize workforce performance, and achieve long-term success.

In the competitive landscape of modern business, organizations that harness the power of HR data will not only survive but thrive. The key lies in understanding what to measure, why it matters, and how to act on the insights gained.

Chapter 10: Using HR KPIs for Continuous Improvement and Adaptation

In the modern business landscape, adaptability and continuous improvement are essential to remain competitive and achieve long-term success. Human Resources (HR) Key Performance Indicators (KPIs) are not merely tools for tracking performance; they are critical in identifying opportunities for growth, addressing challenges, and fostering a culture of innovation. By consistently analyzing HR metrics, organizations can refine their strategies, optimize workforce management, and stay ahead of industry trends.

This chapter delves into how HR KPIs can be leveraged to create a feedback loop of improvement and adaptation, ensuring the organization remains dynamic and resilient in a rapidly changing environment.

The Need for Continuous Improvement in HR

In a world where industries evolve rapidly, businesses must prioritize continuous improvement to thrive. HR functions are central to this process, as the workforce is the foundation of any organization's success. By using HR KPIs, companies can identify inefficiencies, uncover untapped potential, and address emerging workforce needs.

Key Benefits of Continuous Improvement in HR:

1. **Increased Employee Engagement**: Regularly refining HR processes boosts morale and creates an environment where employees feel valued and supported.
2. **Enhanced Productivity**: Optimized strategies improve operational efficiency, resulting in better outcomes for the organization.
3. **Stronger Competitive Edge**: Proactive adaptation allows companies to respond swiftly to market demands and challenges.

Leveraging HR KPIs for Adaptation

Adaptation is the ability to pivot and align organizational strategies with external and internal changes. HR KPIs provide the data necessary to anticipate trends and adjust accordingly.

Steps to Use HR KPIs for Adaptation:

1. **Monitor External Trends:**

- Track industry benchmarks and labor market changes.
- Use KPIs like "Diversity Rate" and "Compensation Competitiveness" to ensure alignment with market standards.

2. **Evaluate Internal Performance:**
   - Analyze metrics such as "Employee Satisfaction Index" and "Attrition Rate" to identify areas needing improvement.
   - Use feedback from KPIs to refine training programs and engagement initiatives.

3. **Implement Agile Workforce Strategies:**
   - Develop flexible policies based on KPI insights, such as remote work trends or evolving employee preferences.
   - Regularly update HR practices to align with shifting organizational goals.

Creating a Feedback Loop with HR KPIs

A feedback loop ensures that the organization consistently learns and improves. HR KPIs play a vital role in creating this loop by providing actionable data for evaluation and refinement.

Components of a Feedback Loop:

1. **Data Collection:**

- Gather accurate and reliable data using metrics like "Training Effectiveness" and "Employee Engagement Rate."

2. **Analysis:**
   - Identify patterns and trends within the data to pinpoint successes and areas for improvement.

3. **Implementation:**
   - Apply insights from KPI analysis to update policies, processes, and strategies.

4. **Review:**
   - Regularly reassess the changes to ensure they meet desired outcomes and adjust as necessary.

Challenges in Using HR KPIs for Continuous Improvement

While HR KPIs offer valuable insights, there are challenges in using them effectively for continuous improvement. These include:

1. **Data Overload:**
   - Too much data can be overwhelming. Focus on key metrics that align with strategic goals.

2. **Resistance to Change:**

- Employees and management may resist new policies or practices. Clear communication and engagement are essential to overcome this hurdle.

3. Ensuring Data Integrity:
- Reliable data collection and analysis are critical. Invest in robust HR technologies to maintain accuracy.

Best Practices for Using HR KPIs in Continuous Improvement

1. Set Clear Objectives:
- Define what the organization wants to achieve with its HR KPIs.

2. Engage Stakeholders:
- Involve employees, managers, and leadership in the KPI tracking process to ensure buy-in and alignment.

3. Utilize Technology:
- Leverage HR analytics tools to automate data collection and analysis for more accurate insights.

4. Focus on Actionable Insights:
- Prioritize KPIs that provide practical information for immediate improvements.

5. **Review Regularly:**
   - Conduct periodic reviews to ensure the continuous relevance and effectiveness of KPIs.

The Future of HR KPIs in Continuous Improvement

As businesses embrace digital transformation, the role of HR KPIs will continue to evolve. Advanced analytics, artificial intelligence, and predictive modeling will further enhance the ability to track, analyze, and act on HR data. By staying ahead of technological advancements, organizations can ensure their HR strategies remain agile and impactful.

Emerging Trends:

- **Predictive Analytics:** Anticipate future workforce needs using advanced data modeling.
- **Employee Experience Metrics:** Focus on holistic measures that capture the overall employee journey.
- **Sustainability KPIs:** Incorporate metrics that align HR practices with environmental and social governance goals.

Conclusion

HR KPIs are powerful tools for driving continuous improvement and fostering adaptability. By leveraging these metrics, organizations can create a resilient workforce, refine their strategies, and achieve sustainable growth. The key lies in maintaining a proactive approach, embracing innovation, and using data-driven insights to navigate the ever-changing business landscape.

Chapter 11: Common Challenges in Implementing HR KPIs and How to Overcome Them

While HR KPIs are invaluable for driving organizational success, implementing and maintaining them effectively comes with its own set of challenges. These challenges can range from technical issues such as ensuring data accuracy to broader concerns like aligning KPIs with business goals and safeguarding employee privacy. Overcoming these obstacles is essential to unlock the full potential of HR KPIs and harness their ability to guide strategic decision-making.

This chapter explores common challenges associated with HR KPIs and provides actionable strategies to address them, ensuring they serve as reliable tools for continuous improvement.

1. Ensuring Data Accuracy and Consistency

One of the most significant challenges in implementing HR KPIs is ensuring that the data collected is accurate, up-to-date, and consistent. Without reliable data, the insights derived from KPIs can lead to flawed conclusions, which may harm decision-making.

Strategies to Overcome:

- **Standardize Data Collection Processes:** Use uniform methods and tools across all departments to collect HR data.

- **Regular Audits:** Conduct periodic reviews of data to identify and correct discrepancies.

- **Invest in Technology:** Use reliable HR software that automates data collection and reduces manual errors.

2. Aligning KPIs with Business Goals

Another common challenge is the misalignment of HR KPIs with broader organizational objectives. When KPIs do not reflect the company's priorities, they become less meaningful and can lead to a disconnect between HR activities and overall business success.

Strategies to Overcome:

- **Collaborate with Leadership:** Work closely with executives to understand the company's strategic goals and tailor HR KPIs to support these objectives.

- **Regular Reviews:** Periodically assess the relevance of HR KPIs to ensure they remain aligned with changing business priorities.
- **Develop Cascading Goals:** Ensure that individual, team, and departmental KPIs feed into overarching organizational goals.

3. Addressing Employee Privacy Concerns

The collection and use of HR data often raise privacy concerns among employees. Ensuring compliance with legal standards and fostering trust is critical for successful KPI implementation.

Strategies to Overcome:

- **Communicate Transparently:** Clearly explain what data is being collected, why, and how it will be used.
- **Comply with Legal Regulations:** Adhere to data protection laws such as GDPR or CCPA, depending on the jurisdiction.
- **Anonymize Data:** Where possible, use aggregated or anonymized data to protect individual identities.

4. Avoiding KPI Overload

Tracking too many KPIs can lead to information overload, diluting the focus on critical metrics and making it challenging to derive actionable insights.

Strategies to Overcome:

- **Prioritize Key Metrics:** Focus on a manageable number of high-impact KPIs that align with business objectives.
- **Use Dashboards:** Implement user-friendly dashboards that highlight the most important KPIs.
- **Regularly Reevaluate Metrics:** Eliminate metrics that no longer serve a purpose or provide value.

5. Encouraging Stakeholder Buy-In

For HR KPIs to be effective, stakeholders across the organization—from leadership to employees—must understand their importance and actively engage with the data.

Strategies to Overcome:

- **Educate Stakeholders:** Provide training sessions to explain the value and purpose of HR KPIs.
- **Showcase Success Stories:** Highlight instances where KPI insights have led to measurable improvements.
- **Foster Collaboration:** Involve stakeholders in the KPI development process to build ownership and commitment.

6. Ensuring Scalability of KPIs

As organizations grow, their HR needs and priorities evolve. Ensuring that KPIs remain scalable and relevant is crucial for long-term success.

Strategies to Overcome:

- **Design Flexible Metrics:** Create KPIs that can be adjusted as the organization expands or shifts focus.
- **Integrate Scalable Technology:** Use HR systems that can handle increasing data volumes and complexity.
- **Anticipate Future Needs:** Regularly assess emerging trends and adjust KPIs to stay ahead of industry changes.

7. Balancing Quantitative and Qualitative Data

Over-reliance on quantitative data can sometimes overlook the nuances captured by qualitative insights, such as employee feedback and cultural observations.

Strategies to Overcome:

- **Combine Data Types:** Use both quantitative metrics and qualitative insights for a comprehensive view.
- **Conduct Surveys and Interviews:** Regularly gather employee opinions to supplement numerical data.
- **Analyze Trends Holistically:** Look for patterns that integrate both numerical and anecdotal evidence.

Conclusion

Implementing HR KPIs effectively requires overcoming challenges related to data accuracy, alignment with business goals, privacy, and scalability, among others. By adopting proactive strategies to address these issues, organizations can ensure their KPIs provide meaningful insights that drive continuous improvement and strategic decision-making. Ultimately, a well-implemented HR KPI framework not only enhances workforce management but also contributes to the overall health and success of the business.

Chapter 12: Future Trends: The Evolving Role of HR KPIs in Business Health

As businesses continue to navigate a rapidly changing landscape, the role of HR KPIs is also evolving to meet new challenges and opportunities. From advancements in technology to shifting workplace expectations, HR KPIs are becoming more sophisticated and integral to strategic planning. This chapter explores the future of HR KPIs, focusing on emerging trends and their potential impact on business health.

1. The Rise of Artificial Intelligence and Automation

Artificial intelligence (AI) and automation are revolutionizing HR processes, enabling businesses to gather, analyze, and act on data more efficiently than ever before. These technologies enhance the accuracy and speed of KPI tracking, providing deeper insights into workforce dynamics.

Key Developments:

- **Predictive Analytics:** AI tools can forecast trends like employee turnover or future hiring needs, allowing businesses to take preemptive action.
- **Automated Reporting:** Automation simplifies the generation of KPI reports, reducing manual effort and minimizing errors.
- **Real-Time Monitoring:** AI-driven systems enable real-time tracking of KPIs, providing instant insights for timely decision-making.

What This Means for Businesses:

By leveraging AI and automation, organizations can gain a competitive edge through enhanced decision-making and operational efficiency.

2. Integrating Employee Experience Metrics

As the focus on employee experience (EX) grows, HR KPIs are expanding to include metrics that capture the holistic well-being and satisfaction of the workforce. These new KPIs go beyond traditional measures to encompass mental health, work-life balance, and overall happiness.

Key Developments:

- **Well-Being KPIs:** Metrics like stress levels, burnout rates, and employee wellness program participation are gaining prominence.
- **Feedback Loops:** Continuous feedback mechanisms, such as pulse surveys, help track employee sentiment in real time.
- **Customizable Metrics:** Businesses are tailoring KPIs to reflect their unique culture and employee priorities.

What This Means for Businesses:

By prioritizing EX metrics, organizations can create a more engaged, productive, and loyal workforce.

3. Emphasis on Diversity, Equity, and Inclusion (DEI)

Diversity, equity, and inclusion are no longer optional—they are critical components of a healthy workplace. HR KPIs are evolving to measure DEI progress more effectively, helping organizations build inclusive cultures.

Key Developments:

- **Expanded DEI Metrics:** KPIs now include measures like demographic representation, pay equity, and inclusion index scores.
- **Intersectional Analysis:** Advanced tools allow businesses to analyze data across multiple dimensions, such as gender, race, and age.

- **Accountability Frameworks:** Organizations are using DEI KPIs to hold leadership accountable for progress.

What This Means for Businesses:

By embracing DEI-focused KPIs, companies can foster innovation, attract top talent, and enhance their reputation.

4. The Role of People Analytics

People analytics is becoming a cornerstone of HR strategy, combining data science and human insights to inform KPI development and application. This approach enables businesses to make evidence-based decisions about their workforce.

Key Developments:

- **Advanced Dashboards:** Interactive dashboards provide a comprehensive view of HR metrics, making it easier to identify trends and areas for improvement.
- **Data Integration:** Combining data from multiple sources, such as HR software, surveys, and performance reviews, creates a more complete picture.
- **Customized Insights:** Analytics tools are tailoring recommendations based on specific business contexts.

What This Means for Businesses:

People analytics empowers leaders to act with confidence, ensuring that HR strategies align with broader organizational goals.

5. Focus on Sustainability and Corporate Responsibility

As sustainability becomes a core business priority, HR KPIs are beginning to reflect an organization's commitment to environmental and social responsibility. These metrics demonstrate how HR initiatives contribute to sustainable practices.

Key Developments:

- **Green Initiatives:** Tracking participation in environmentally friendly programs, such as remote work policies or green commuting options.
- **Community Engagement:** Measuring employee involvement in volunteering and corporate social responsibility projects.
- **Sustainable Workforce Planning:** Ensuring long-term workforce sustainability through strategic hiring and development.

What This Means for Businesses:

By incorporating sustainability metrics into HR KPIs, companies can align their workforce strategies with global trends and consumer expectations.

6. Increasing Personalization of KPIs

One-size-fits-all approaches to KPIs are being replaced by personalized metrics that account for individual roles, teams, and business units. This customization enhances the relevance and impact of HR KPIs.

Key Developments:

- **Role-Specific KPIs:** Metrics tailored to specific job functions provide more actionable insights.
- **Team-Level Metrics:** Tracking performance at the team level helps identify group dynamics and collaboration opportunities.
- **Employee-Centric Dashboards:** Personalized dashboards allow employees to view and track their own KPIs.

What This Means for Businesses:

Personalized KPIs drive engagement and accountability by making performance metrics more meaningful to individuals.

7. Embracing Remote and Hybrid Work Models

The shift to remote and hybrid work has transformed how businesses measure workforce performance. HR KPIs are adapting to assess productivity, engagement, and collaboration in distributed environments.

Key Developments:

- **Remote Work Metrics:** KPIs like virtual meeting attendance, remote task completion rates, and digital collaboration scores are becoming standard.
- **Flexibility Indicators:** Tracking flexible work adoption rates and employee satisfaction with remote policies.

- **Technology Utilization:** Measuring the effectiveness of tools and platforms that support remote work.

What This Means for Businesses:

By refining KPIs for remote and hybrid work, organizations can optimize these models while maintaining high performance and engagement.

8. The Growing Importance of Predictive and Prescriptive Analytics

Predictive and prescriptive analytics are transforming HR KPIs from retrospective tools to proactive strategies. These advanced analytics methods provide insights into future trends and recommend actionable steps.

Key Developments:

- **Turnover Predictions:** Identifying employees at risk of leaving and implementing retention strategies.
- **Skill Gap Analysis:** Forecasting future skill needs and aligning training programs accordingly.
- **Scenario Planning:** Simulating the impact of HR decisions on business outcomes.

What This Means for Businesses:

Predictive and prescriptive analytics enable companies to stay ahead of challenges, ensuring their workforce strategies remain agile and effective.

Conclusion

The future of HR KPIs is dynamic and data-driven, shaped by technological advancements, changing workforce expectations, and global trends. By staying attuned to these developments, businesses can leverage HR KPIs to foster innovation, enhance employee satisfaction, and drive sustainable growth. Embracing the evolving role of HR KPIs ensures that organizations remain competitive and resilient in an ever-changing world.

Conclusion: The Critical Role of HR KPIs in Shaping a Successful Business

As we conclude this exploration of HR Key Performance Indicators (KPIs), it becomes clear that these metrics are not merely numbers on a dashboard—they are critical tools that shape the trajectory of a successful business. By integrating HR KPIs into strategic decision-making, organizations can unlock a wealth of insights that drive growth, improve employee well-being, and create a resilient, adaptable workforce. This chapter ties together the key themes discussed throughout the book and emphasizes the necessity of embracing HR KPIs as a cornerstone of business health.

The Transformative Power of HR KPIs

HR KPIs are far more than administrative tools; they are transformative agents that align human resources with organizational goals. By tracking and analyzing these metrics, companies gain a deeper understanding of their workforce, uncovering opportunities for improvement and innovation.

Key Benefits of HR KPIs:

- **Enhanced Decision-Making:** HR KPIs provide data-driven insights that support informed strategic choices.
- **Increased Transparency:** Metrics ensure accountability and clarity in HR processes.
- **Proactive Problem-Solving:** Early identification of trends allows businesses to address issues before they escalate.

Organizations that prioritize HR KPIs can adapt to change more effectively and maintain a competitive edge in their industry.

Reinforcing Employee Engagement and Satisfaction

One of the most compelling reasons to implement HR KPIs is their impact on employee engagement and satisfaction. A satisfied, engaged workforce is the foundation of a successful business, and KPIs help organizations measure and enhance these critical areas.

Practical Applications:

- Use **Employee Net Promoter Scores (eNPS)** to gauge loyalty and advocacy among staff.
- Track **survey participation rates** to ensure employee voices are heard.
- Monitor **retention metrics** to identify trends in turnover and develop targeted retention strategies.

Engaged employees are more productive, innovative, and committed to achieving organizational goals, making these KPIs indispensable.

Optimizing Recruitment and Retention

Recruitment and retention are two sides of the same coin, and HR KPIs bridge the gap between attracting top talent and keeping them engaged. Metrics like **time to hire** and **cost per hire** ensure that recruitment strategies are efficient and cost-effective.

Key Strategies for Success:

- Regularly review **turnover rates** to understand the reasons behind employee departures.
- Utilize **candidate experience scores** to refine recruitment processes.
- Align **onboarding satisfaction metrics** with retention goals.

By leveraging these KPIs, businesses can build a stable and motivated workforce.

Continuous Learning and Development

A culture of continuous learning is vital for long-term business success. HR KPIs related to training and development provide insights into the effectiveness of learning programs and their impact on employee performance.

How to Measure Impact:

- Track **training completion rates** to ensure participation.
- Analyze **post-training performance improvements** to measure skill acquisition.
- Monitor **career progression metrics** to assess the effectiveness of development initiatives.

Investing in employee growth leads to a more skilled, confident, and capable workforce, driving innovation and adaptability.

Driving Diversity and Inclusion (D&I)

Diversity and inclusion are no longer optional—they are essential for fostering innovation and maintaining relevance in a global market. HR KPIs help businesses measure their progress in creating inclusive environments.

Effective Metrics:

- **Representation metrics** track demographic diversity across all levels of the organization.
- **Pay equity analysis** ensures fair compensation practices.

- **Inclusion surveys** provide insights into employee perceptions of workplace equity.

By prioritizing D&I-focused KPIs, organizations can create a culture that values diversity and empowers all employees to succeed.

Adapting to Future Trends

The future of HR KPIs lies in embracing emerging technologies and trends that enhance their effectiveness. From artificial intelligence to predictive analytics, the tools available for tracking and analyzing KPIs are evolving rapidly.

Key Areas to Watch:

- **AI and Automation:** Streamlining data collection and analysis.
- **Predictive Analytics:** Anticipating trends and preparing for workforce changes.
- **Employee Experience Metrics:** Measuring holistic well-being and satisfaction.

By staying ahead of these trends, businesses can ensure their HR strategies remain relevant and impactful.

A Call to Action for Business Leaders

The journey to leveraging HR KPIs effectively begins with a commitment to data-driven decision-making. Leaders must prioritize the integration of HR metrics into their strategic planning processes and foster a culture that values transparency and continuous improvement.

Steps to Get Started:

1. **Identify Key Metrics:** Focus on the KPIs most relevant to your business goals.
2. **Invest in Technology:** Implement tools that simplify data collection and analysis.
3. **Regularly Review Metrics:** Make KPI reviews a standard part of strategic discussions.
4. **Engage Employees:** Involve staff in developing and refining metrics to ensure buy-in.

By taking these steps, organizations can unlock the full potential of HR KPIs and achieve sustainable success.

Conclusion

HR KPIs are indispensable tools for measuring and improving the health of a business. They provide a clear picture of workforce dynamics, uncover opportunities for growth, and enable data-driven decision-making. By embracing these metrics and adapting to emerging trends, organizations can create a thriving workplace that supports both employees and business objectives. The future of HR KPIs is bright, and the time to act is now. Business leaders must seize this opportunity to shape a successful, sustainable, and inclusive future.

Appendix: 40 KPIs To Use

COMPENSATION KPI'S (7)

These KPIs focus on evaluating the financial aspects of workforce management. They measure the cost effectiveness and competitiveness of employee compensation, benefits, and productivity.

Evaluating the Competitiveness of Compensation Options:

Evaluating the competitiveness of compensation options involves analyzing whether your organization's pay structure aligns with market standards. This process ensures that salaries offered are attractive enough to retain and recruit top talent while remaining sustainable for the business. By comparing internal pay rates to industry averages, companies can identify gaps in their compensation strategy, address inequities, and strengthen their employer value proposition. A competitive salary package enhances employee satisfaction, motivation, and loyalty, ultimately contributing to organizational success. The Salary Competitiveness Ratio (SCR) serves as a key metric to quantify how well compensation aligns with market norms.

Formula for Salary Competitiveness Ratio (SCR):

$$SCR = \frac{\text{Average Employee Salary}}{\text{Market Average Salary}} \times 100$$

Measuring the Workforce Cost Against Total Company Costs Within a Period:

Measuring the percentage of labor cost involves assessing the proportion of total organizational expenses dedicated to workforce-related expenditures, including salaries, benefits, and other employee-related costs. This metric provides insight into how efficiently a company is allocating its financial resources toward its workforce compared to other operational costs. By tracking this percentage over time, organizations can identify trends, evaluate the sustainability of labor costs, and make strategic adjustments to maintain profitability. Understanding labor costs relative to total company costs is essential for financial planning, benchmarking, and ensuring long-term organizational health.

Formula for Percentage of Labor Cost:

$$\text{Percentage of Labor Cost} = \left(\frac{\text{Total Labor Cost}}{\text{Total Company Costs}}\right) \times 100$$

Assessing the Company's Healthcare Plan Comprehensiveness:

Assessing a company's healthcare plan comprehensiveness involves evaluating the scope, quality, and affordability of the health benefits provided to employees. This includes analyzing coverage options, cost-sharing structures, and the overall financial impact of the healthcare plan on the organization and its workforce. The KPI for Healthcare Costs per Employee helps organizations determine whether their health benefits align with employee needs and industry benchmarks. A well-structured healthcare plan not only promotes employee well-being and satisfaction but also enhances recruitment and retention efforts. Regular assessment ensures the plan remains competitive and sustainable while meeting compliance requirements.

Formula for Healthcare Costs per Employee:

$$\text{Healthcare Costs per Employee} = \frac{\text{Total Healthcare Costs}}{\text{Number of Employees}}$$

Benefits Satisfaction:

Benefits satisfaction measures how well an organization's benefits package meets the needs and expectations of its employees. This KPI is derived from employee feedback, typically collected through surveys or focus groups, and reflects the perceived value and adequacy of offerings such as healthcare, retirement plans, paid time off, and other perks. High benefits satisfaction indicates that employees feel supported and valued, which can boost morale, productivity, and retention. Regularly assessing benefits satisfaction enables organizations to identify areas for improvement and ensure their benefits remain competitive and aligned with workforce priorities.

Formula for Benefits Satisfaction:

$$\text{Benefits Satisfaction} = \left(\frac{\text{Number of Employees Satisfied with Benefits}}{\text{Total Number of Employees Surveyed}}\right) \times 100$$

Description of Employee Productivity Rate:

The Employee Productivity Rate measures workforce efficiency by evaluating the output generated relative to the resources invested, such as employee count or hours worked, over a specific period. This KPI provides insights into how effectively employees contribute to achieving organizational goals. A higher productivity rate indicates that the workforce is performing efficiently, maximizing results with minimal waste of resources. Tracking this metric over time helps identify trends, pinpoint inefficiencies, and develop strategies to enhance overall performance through training, process improvements, or resource allocation adjustments.

Formula for Employee Productivity Rate:

$$\text{Employee Productivity Rate} = \frac{\text{Total Output (e.g., Revenue, Units Produced)}}{\text{Total Input (e.g., Number of Employees, Hours Worked)}}$$

Evaluating the Profitability of Investing in Employee Training:

Return on Investment (ROI) in employee training measures the financial impact of training programs by comparing the benefits gained against the costs incurred. This metric helps organizations determine whether their training initiatives effectively contribute to profitability and performance improvements. By evaluating ROI, businesses can identify which training programs provide the most value, ensure strategic alignment with organizational goals, and make data-driven decisions about future investments. A positive ROI indicates that the training has successfully enhanced employee skills, productivity, or efficiency, leading to tangible organizational benefits.

Formula for Return on Investment (ROI) in Employee Training:

$$ROI = \left(\frac{\text{Net Benefits from Training} - \text{Training Costs}}{\text{Training Costs}}\right) \times 100$$

Where:

- **Net Benefits from Training** = Measurable gains from training (e.g., increased revenue, reduced costs)
- **Training Costs** = Total investment in the training program (e.g., materials, trainer fees, time).

EMPLOYEE PERFORMANCE KPIs (7)

These KPIs assess the effectiveness of the organization in managing employee performance and development. They help in understanding how internal processes contribute to overall workforce productivity and career progression.

Comparing New Hires' Performance to Other Employees:

The Performance of New Hires KPI evaluates how new employees perform relative to the overall workforce. By comparing the average performance scores of new hires to those of existing employees, this metric provides insights into the effectiveness of recruitment, onboarding, and training processes. A high percentage indicates that new hires are quickly acclimating and contributing to organizational goals, while a lower percentage may highlight gaps in hiring criteria or integration strategies. Tracking this KPI helps organizations refine their talent acquisition and development practices to ensure sustained workforce quality and productivity.

Formula for Performance of New Hires:

$$\text{Performance of New Hires} = \frac{\text{Average Performance Score of New Hires}}{\text{Average Performance Score of All Employees}} \times 100$$

Internal Promotion Rate:

The Internal Promotion Rate measures the organization's success in advancing internal talent into higher roles. This KPI reflects the effectiveness of career development programs, talent management strategies, and succession planning within the company. A high internal promotion rate indicates a commitment to employee growth, which can enhance morale, engagement, and retention. Conversely, a low rate may signal a need for improved training, development opportunities, or clearer career pathways. Monitoring this metric helps organizations assess their ability to nurture and leverage internal talent to meet evolving business needs.

Formula for Internal Promotion Rate:

$$\text{Internal Promotion Rate} = \left(\frac{\text{Number of Internal Promotions}}{\text{Total Number of Employees}}\right) \times 100$$

Employee Engagement in Business Process Improvement:

The Suggestions per Employee KPI measures the extent of employee involvement in generating ideas to enhance business processes, products, or services. This metric reflects the level of engagement, innovation, and willingness of employees to contribute beyond their regular duties. A higher rate of suggestions indicates a culture that encourages collaboration and values employee input, leading to continuous improvement and innovation. Tracking this KPI helps organizations identify opportunities to strengthen communication channels, recognize contributors, and implement ideas that drive operational and strategic success.

Formula for Suggestions per Employee:

$$\text{Suggestions per Employee} = \frac{\text{Total Number of Suggestions Submitted}}{\text{Total Number of Employees}}$$

HR Full-Time Equivalents (FTEs) Relative to Total Employees:

The HR to Employee Ratio measures the number of human resources staff (full-time equivalents) available to support a defined number of employees within an organization. This KPI provides insight into the adequacy of HR resources in relation to workforce size. A lower ratio may indicate a lean HR structure, potentially affecting service delivery and employee support, while a higher ratio suggests more robust HR support. Monitoring this metric helps organizations assess their HR capacity, optimize resource allocation, and ensure the effective management of employee needs, compliance, and strategic initiatives.

Formula for HR to Employee Ratio:

$$\text{HR to Employee Ratio} = \frac{\text{Number of HR Full-Time Equivalents (FTEs)}}{\text{Total Number of Employees}} \times 1000$$

(The ratio is often expressed per 1,000 employees.)

Timeframe for Payroll Processing:

Cycle Time to Process Payroll measures the amount of time required to complete payroll activities from start to finish for a given payroll period. This KPI helps organizations track the efficiency and effectiveness of payroll processing systems, ensuring timely and accurate compensation for employees. A shorter cycle time reflects an optimized process, while longer times may indicate inefficiencies or bottlenecks that could affect employee satisfaction and compliance with payroll deadlines. Monitoring this metric enables businesses to streamline payroll workflows, reduce administrative burdens, and ensure employees are paid accurately and on time.

Formula for Cycle Time to Process Payroll:

$$\text{Cycle Time to Process Payroll} = \frac{\text{Total Time Spent on Payroll Processing}}{\text{Number of Payroll Periods}}$$

(Time is typically measured in hours or days per payroll period.)

Tracking Low-Performing Employees:

The Percentage of Workforce Below Performance Standards KPI tracks the proportion of employees who are not meeting established performance expectations. This metric helps organizations identify areas where additional support, training, or interventions may be needed to improve employee performance. A high percentage may signal issues with training, unclear performance expectations, or other factors affecting employee productivity. Regularly tracking this KPI enables businesses to take timely corrective actions, such as coaching or performance improvement plans, to align employees with organizational goals and improve overall performance.

Formula for Percentage of Workforce Below Performance Standards:

$$\text{Percentage of Workforce Below Performance Standards} = \left(\frac{\text{Number of Employees Below Performance Standards}}{\text{Total Number of Employees}}\right) \times 100$$

Internal Job Hire Rate:

The Internal Job Hire Rate measures the proportion of positions filled by existing employees as opposed to external candidates. This KPI highlights the success of internal talent development, promotion, and career progression initiatives within the organization. A higher rate indicates that the organization is effectively nurturing and retaining its talent, providing growth opportunities and fostering employee loyalty. Conversely, a lower rate may suggest limited internal development or a reliance on external hires for skills that could be cultivated within. Tracking this metric supports strategic workforce planning and reinforces the value of internal mobility for organizational success.

Formula for Internal Job Hire Rate:

$$\text{Internal Job Hire Rate} = \left(\frac{\text{Number of Internal Hires}}{\text{Total Number of Hires}}\right) \times 100$$

EMPLOYEE EXPERIENCE KPIs (7)

These KPIs focus on the overall employee experience, including satisfaction, engagement with company culture, and work-life balance, reflecting the organization's environment and culture.

Employee Satisfaction Index:

The Employee Satisfaction Index measures the overall happiness and contentment of employees within an organization. This KPI is typically derived from employee surveys that assess various aspects of the work environment, such as compensation, benefits, management, work-life balance, and career development opportunities. A higher Employee Satisfaction Index indicates a more engaged and satisfied workforce, which can lead to improved productivity, reduced turnover, and better organizational performance. Regularly tracking this metric helps companies understand employee sentiment, identify areas for improvement, and take proactive steps to enhance the work experience.

Formula for Employee Satisfaction Index:

$$\text{Employee Satisfaction Index} = \frac{\text{Sum of Employee Satisfaction Scores}}{\text{Total Number of Employees Surveyed}}$$

(The satisfaction scores are typically gathered through employee surveys, often on a scale from 1 to 5 or 1 to 10.)

Number of Employee Satisfaction Surveys:

The Number of Employee Satisfaction Surveys KPI tracks how frequently an organization conducts surveys to measure employee happiness, engagement, and satisfaction. This metric reflects the company's commitment to understanding its employees' needs and continuously improving the work environment. Regularly gathering employee feedback through surveys shows that the organization values input and is proactive in maintaining or improving employee well-being. A higher number of surveys can indicate a strong focus on fostering a positive work culture, addressing employee concerns, and making data-driven decisions to enhance job satisfaction and retention.

Formula for Number of Employee Satisfaction Surveys:

$$\text{Number of Employee Satisfaction Surveys} = \text{Total Number of Surveys Conducted in a Given Period}$$

Percentage of Employees Trained in Company Culture:

The Percentage of Employees Trained in Company Culture KPI measures the proportion of employees who have received training or orientation related to the organization's values, mission, and cultural norms. This metric helps evaluate how well employees understand and align with the company's culture. A higher percentage indicates that the company is successful in instilling its cultural values across the workforce, which can enhance employee engagement, communication, and overall job satisfaction. Regular training in company culture is essential for fostering a cohesive, unified workforce that contributes to the long-term success and sustainability of the organization.

Formula for Percentage of Employees Trained in Company Culture:

$$\text{Percentage of Employees Trained in Company Culture} = \left(\frac{\text{Number of Employees Trained in Company Culture}}{\text{Total Number of Employees}} \right) \times 100$$

Percentage of Vacation Days Used:

The Percentage of Vacation Days Used KPI measures the extent to which employees take advantage of the vacation days allotted to them. This metric provides insights into employees' attitudes toward work-life balance and their willingness to disconnect from work. A high percentage may indicate that employees value time off and prioritize personal well-being, contributing to reduced burnout and improved productivity. Conversely, a low percentage could suggest that employees are not fully utilizing their benefits, possibly due to workload pressure or a company culture that discourages time off. Tracking this KPI helps organizations ensure their workforce maintains a healthy work-life balance, ultimately enhancing long-term employee engagement and retention.

Formula for Percentage of Vacation Days Used:

$$\text{Percentage of Vacation Days Used} = \left(\frac{\text{Total Vacation Days Taken by Employees}}{\text{Total Vacation Days Available to Employees}} \right) \times 100$$

Employee Net Promoter Score (eNPS):

The Employee Net Promoter Score (eNPS) measures the likelihood of employees recommending their organization to others as a great place to work. This KPI provides a clear gauge of overall employee satisfaction and engagement. A positive eNPS indicates that employees are enthusiastic and willing to promote the company, reflecting a healthy work culture and high job satisfaction. A negative score, on the other hand, suggests that there may be underlying issues, such as low morale or dissatisfaction. Regularly tracking eNPS helps organizations assess their employee experience, identify areas for improvement, and implement strategies to strengthen employee loyalty and retention.

Formula for Employee Net Promoter Score (eNPS):

$$eNPS = \%\text{Promoters} - \%\text{Detractors}$$

Where:

- **Promoters** are employees who rate their likelihood of recommending the company as 9 or 10 on a scale from 0 to 10.

- **Detractors** are employees who rate their likelihood of recommending the company as 0 to 6.

- **Passives** are those who rate their likelihood as 7 or 8 but are not considered in the final calculation.

Average Tenure:

The Average Tenure KPI measures the average length of time employees stay with the organization. It provides insight into employee retention, organizational stability, and the effectiveness of employee engagement strategies. A longer average tenure typically indicates that employees are satisfied, loyal, and committed to the company's values and goals. Conversely, a shorter average tenure might suggest higher turnover, which could be caused by factors like job dissatisfaction, lack of career advancement, or a challenging work environment. By tracking this metric, companies can assess the effectiveness of their retention efforts, identify trends in employee loyalty, and make improvements to enhance long-term employee satisfaction.

Formula for Average Tenure:

$$\text{Average Tenure} = \frac{\text{Total Years of Service of All Employees}}{\text{Total Number of Employees}}$$

Learning & Development Score:

The Learning & Development Score measures employee satisfaction with the organization's development and education opportunities. This KPI helps evaluate how well employees perceive the effectiveness and accessibility of training programs, career development resources, and skill-building initiatives. A higher score indicates that employees feel supported in their growth and believe that the organization invests in their professional development. Conversely, a lower score suggests that there may be gaps in the available training or a lack of clear opportunities for advancement. By monitoring this metric, organizations can assess and improve their learning and development strategies, ensuring employees have the tools and resources to advance their careers.

Formula for Learning & Development Score:

$$\text{Learning \& Development Score} = \frac{\text{Sum of Employee Satisfaction Scores on T \& D}}{\text{Total Number of Employees Surveyed}}$$

(Employee satisfaction scores are typically gathered through surveys on a scale from 1 to 5 or 1 to 10, assessing aspects like training quality, relevance, and accessibility.)

IMPLEMENTING AND MANAGING HR KPIs (6)

Select Relevant KPIs. Choose KPIs that align with your organization's specific goals and challenges. Net all KPIs will be relevant for every company.

Reliable Data Sources:

The Reliable Data Sources KPI evaluates the accuracy, consistency, and timeliness of the data used to calculate HR metrics and KPIs. Accurate and consistent data is crucial for maintaining the integrity of HR analyses and ensuring informed decision-making. Using unreliable or inconsistent data can lead to incorrect conclusions, impacting the effectiveness of talent management strategies, workforce planning, and employee engagement efforts. This metric emphasizes the importance of leveraging trusted, high-quality data from verified sources—such as HRIS systems, performance tracking tools, and employee surveys—to provide a clear, accurate view of key workforce metrics. Maintaining reliable data sources enables organizations to make data-driven decisions that align with business goals and enhance overall HR performance.

Formula for Reliable Data Sources:

$$\text{Reliability Score} = \left(\frac{\text{Number of Accurate Data Entries}}{\text{Total Data Entries}} \right) \times 100$$

There isn't a single formula for this KPI, but it is typically evaluated based on the accuracy, consistency, and timeliness of the data used to calculate HR metrics. A possible approach could be:

Align with Organizational Goals. Ensure that HR KPIs are aligned with the broader business strategy and objectives.

Learn from Analysis:

The "Learn from Analysis" KPI measures how effectively the organization uses the insights derived from HR data analysis to drive strategic decisions and continuous improvement. By regularly evaluating HR KPIs and identifying patterns or trends, organizations can make informed decisions to enhance talent management, improve employee engagement, optimize operations, and drive business growth. This KPI emphasizes the importance of not only collecting data but also acting on it. For example, if employee turnover data highlights a potential issue in retention, the company can take targeted actions, such as enhancing development programs or adjusting compensation strategies. Continuously learning from data helps organizations stay agile, adapt to changes, and ensure that HR strategies align with broader business objectives.

Formula for Learn from Analysis:

There isn't a single fixed formula for this KPI, as it focuses on interpreting the results from HR analytics and using those insights to drive continuous improvement. However, it can be assessed using the following approach:

$$\text{Learn from Analysis Score} = \left(\frac{\text{Number of Actionable Insights Taken from KPIs}}{\text{Total Number of KPIs Analyzed}} \right) \times 100$$

Holistic Approach:

The "Holistic Approach" KPI emphasizes the value of combining both quantitative (hard) data and qualitative (soft) insights to create a well-rounded view of HR performance. While hard data offers measurable metrics, such as turnover rates, productivity levels, or compensation benchmarks, qualitative insights provide context by capturing employee sentiment, engagement, and perceptions. By integrating these two types of data, organizations can gain a deeper understanding of HR outcomes, allowing for more informed and effective decision-making. This approach ensures that HR strategies are not solely based on numbers but also account for the human element, leading to a balanced and comprehensive understanding of workforce dynamics and organizational health.

Formula for Holistic Approach:

There isn't a single standard formula for this KPI, as it involves combining multiple data sources for a comprehensive view of HR performance. However, it can be assessed as follows:

$$\text{Holistic Approach Score} = \left(\frac{\text{Hard Data}}{\text{Total Data Points}} + \frac{\text{Qualitative Insights}}{\text{Total Insights}} \right) \times 100$$

Where:

- **Hard Data** refers to quantitative metrics (e.g., employee turnover, performance metrics, etc.).

- **Qualitative Insights** refer to feedback, surveys, and other subjective data (e.g., employee satisfaction, engagement feedback, etc.).

Compliance:

The Compliance KPI focuses on ensuring that all HR activities and KPI tracking methods align with legal standards, particularly concerning employee privacy and other regulatory requirements. This includes safeguarding personal employee data, ensuring fair labor practices, adhering to health and safety regulations, and complying with employment laws such as the Family and Medical Leave Act (FMLA) or Equal Employment Opportunity (EEO) guidelines. A high compliance score indicates that the organization is successfully tracking and managing HR metrics in a legally compliant manner, reducing the risk of legal issues or fines. Maintaining strict compliance not only protects the company but also promotes trust and transparency with employees, ensuring their privacy and rights are respected.

Formula for Compliance:

There isn't a single formula for this KPI, as it involves ensuring adherence to legal standards across HR data tracking and management. However, it can be evaluated based on adherence to regulations:

$$\text{Compliance Score} = \left(\frac{\text{Number of Compliant HR Practices}}{\text{Total Number of HR Practices Audited}} \right) \times 100$$

Where:

- **Number of Compliant HR Practices** refers to the HR activities or data practices that are fully compliant with legal and regulatory standards (e.g., employee privacy laws, wage laws).

- **Total Number of HR Practices Audited** refers to the total HR practices or activities reviewed for compliance.

EMPLOYMENT KPIs (20)

These KPIs track the size and dynamics of the workplace, including aspects of hiring, training, diversity, and employee turnover, reflecting the effectiveness of talent management strategies.

Number of Full-Time Employees:

The "Number of Full-Time Employees" KPI tracks the size and growth of the company's full-time workforce. By monitoring this metric, organizations can gauge their staffing levels and understand how their workforce is evolving over time. An increase in the number of full-time employees typically signals business growth and the need for more dedicated, long-term staff to meet organizational goals. Conversely, a decrease might indicate downsizing or a shift towards part-time or contract workers. This KPI is essential for workforce planning, budgeting, and resource allocation, ensuring that the company has the right number of full-time employees to meet business demands effectively. Tracking this metric can also help assess the effectiveness of recruitment efforts and talent retention strategies.

Formula for Number of Full-Time Employees:

Number of Full-Time Employees=Total Full-Time Employees

Where:

- **Total Full-Time Employees** refers to the number of employees who are classified as full-time based on the company's definition (e.g., employees working 40 hours per week or more).

Number of Employees per Location:

The "Number of Employees per Location" KPI helps organizations monitor and manage the distribution of their workforce across various locations. This metric is valuable for understanding employee work location preferences, whether at a physical office or remotely, and can help inform decisions related to resource allocation, office space utilization, and recruitment strategies. By tracking the number of employees at each location, businesses can assess the impact of location-specific factors such as regional talent availability, employee satisfaction, and operational efficiency. It also aids in workforce planning, ensuring that each location has adequate staffing levels to meet business needs while addressing employee preferences for remote or on-site work.

Formula for Number of Employees per Location:

$$\text{Number of Employees per Location} = \frac{\text{Total Employees at a Specific Location}}{\text{Total Number of Locations}}$$

Where:

- **Total Employees at a Specific Location** refers to the number of employees working at each individual location or office.

- **Total Number of Locations** refers to the total number of different work locations the company operates, such as regional offices, branches, or remote hubs.

Retirement Rate:

The "Retirement Rate" KPI measures the percentage of employees retiring within a given period relative to the total workforce. This metric is crucial for strategic workforce planning as it helps organizations anticipate future staffing needs and manage succession planning effectively. A high retirement rate signals that a significant portion of the workforce may soon exit the organization, creating potential gaps in experience, knowledge, and skills. By tracking the retirement rate, companies can prepare for these changes by developing strategies such as cross-training, knowledge transfer programs, and recruiting new talent to ensure business continuity. Understanding retirement trends also aids in aligning HR practices with long-term business goals and optimizing labor costs.

Formula for Retirement Rate:

$$\text{Retirement Rate} = \frac{\text{Number of Employees Retiring}}{\text{Total Number of Employees}} \times 100$$

Where:

- **Number of Employees Retiring** refers to the employees who retire within a specific time period.
- **Total Number of Employees** refers to the total workforce during the same period.

Average Age of Retirement:

The "Average Age of Retirement" KPI calculates the typical age at which employees retire within an organization. This metric is important for workforce planning as it helps businesses forecast future retirements and prepare for the potential loss of experienced talent. By understanding the average retirement age, companies can proactively implement succession planning and replacement strategies, ensuring that they have a pipeline of skilled employees ready to step into key roles. It also aids in estimating future costs related to pensions, benefits, and retirement packages, and helps HR teams plan for knowledge transfer initiatives to mitigate the impact of retirements on operations and organizational expertise.

Formula for Average Age of Retirement:

$$\text{Average Age of Retirement} = \frac{\sum \text{Age of Employees at Retirement}}{\text{Total Number of Employees Retiring}}$$

Where:

- **Age of Employees at Retirement** refers to the age of each employee when they retire.

- **Total Number of Employees Retiring** refers to the total number of employees who retire in the period being measured.

New Hire 90-Day Failure Rate:

The "New Hire 90-Day Failure Rate" KPI measures the percentage of new employees who leave the company within their first 90 days of employment. This metric is critical for assessing the effectiveness of the talent acquisition and onboarding processes. A high failure rate indicates potential issues in the hiring process, such as mismatched job expectations, inadequate onboarding, or cultural misalignment. By tracking this KPI, HR teams can identify areas for improvement in recruitment strategies, onboarding programs, and employee integration efforts. Reducing the 90-day failure rate is crucial for improving retention, enhancing the candidate selection process, and ensuring that new hires are set up for success in their roles.

Formula for New Hire 90-Day Failure Rate:

$$\text{New Hire 90-Day Failure Rate} = \frac{\text{Number of New Hires Who Leave Within 90 Days}}{\text{Total Number of New Hires}} \times 100$$

Where:

- **Number of New Hires Who Leave Within 90 Days** refers to employees who voluntarily or involuntarily leave the company within the first 90 days of employment.
- **Total Number of New Hires** refers to the total number of new employees hired within the same period.

First Year Voluntary Termination Rate:

The "First Year Voluntary Termination Rate" KPI tracks the percentage of new employees who choose to leave the company voluntarily within their first year. This metric provides valuable insight into how well the company integrates and supports new hires. A high first-year voluntary termination rate may indicate issues with employee engagement, job satisfaction, company culture, or unrealistic job expectations. On the other hand, a low rate suggests that employees are adapting well and finding value in their roles, reflecting a positive work environment. By monitoring this KPI, organizations can identify areas for improvement in onboarding, mentorship, and employee retention strategies, ensuring they provide a welcoming and supportive experience for new hires.

Formula for First Year Voluntary Termination Rate:

$$\text{First Year Voluntary Termination Rate} = \frac{\text{Number of Voluntary Terminations in First Year}}{\text{Total Number of New Hires in the Same Year}} \times 100$$

Where:

- **Number of Voluntary Terminations in First Year** refers to employees who voluntarily leave the company within their first year of employment.
- **Total Number of New Hires in the Same Year** refers to the total number of new employees hired during the same period.

Average Time to Fill a Job Vacancy:

The "Average Time to Fill a Job Vacancy" KPI measures the average number of days it takes to fill an open position within the organization. This metric is crucial for evaluating the efficiency of the hiring process and identifying bottlenecks in recruitment. A shorter time to fill suggests that the company has an effective and streamlined process for sourcing, interviewing, and hiring candidates. Conversely, a longer time to fill may indicate inefficiencies, such as delays in the interview process, unclear job requirements, or challenges in attracting qualified candidates. By monitoring this KPI, HR teams can optimize recruitment strategies, improve candidate experience, and reduce the time it takes to bring in necessary talent, which in turn helps minimize productivity losses and maintain operational continuity.

Formula for Average Time to Fill a Job Vacancy:

$$\text{Average Time to Fill} = \frac{\sum \text{Time to Fill Each Vacancy}}{\text{Total Number of Job Vacancies Filled}}$$

Where:

- **Time to Fill Each Vacancy** refers to the number of days from when a job requisition is approved to when a candidate accepts the offer and is hired.

- **Total Number of Job Vacancies Filled** refers to the total number of positions successfully filled in the given period.

Attrition Rate:

The "Attrition Rate" KPI measures the percentage of employees who leave an organization over a specific period, whether due to voluntary resignation, retirement, or involuntary termination. This metric is essential for evaluating the company's success in retaining talent. A high attrition rate can indicate underlying issues, such as poor employee engagement, dissatisfaction with compensation or benefits, lack of career development opportunities, or an unhealthy work environment. On the other hand, a low attrition rate suggests that the organization is effectively retaining its employees and fostering a positive work culture. By monitoring this KPI, HR teams can identify potential retention challenges, implement targeted interventions to improve employee satisfaction, and reduce the cost and disruption caused by high turnover.

Formula for Attrition Rate:

$$\text{Attrition Rate} = \frac{\text{Number of Employees Who Leave During a Period}}{\text{Average Number of Employees During the Same Period}} \times 100$$

Where:

- **Number of Employees Who Leave During a Period** refers to the total number of employees who voluntarily or involuntarily leave the company during a specific period (e.g., monthly, quarterly, or yearly).

- **Average Number of Employees During the Same Period** is the average number of employees during that same period, calculated by adding the number of employees at the beginning and end of the period and dividing by 2.

Compliance KPI:

The "Compliance" KPI measures how well an organization adheres to legal and regulatory standards, particularly in areas like labor laws, employee privacy, health and safety regulations, and data protection. It ensures that all HR-related activities, such as payroll processing, hiring practices, employee data management, and workplace safety procedures, are compliant with relevant legislation. A high compliance rate reflects that the organization is managing its HR processes effectively and within the bounds of the law, which reduces legal risks and potential penalties. This KPI is particularly important when tracking employee privacy, ensuring that employee data is handled securely and in accordance with laws like GDPR or HIPAA. Regular compliance audits and assessments can help identify any gaps or risks, enabling HR teams to address them proactively and maintain trust and transparency with employees and regulatory bodies.

Formula for Compliance KPI:

$$\text{Compliance Rate} = \frac{\text{Number of Compliant Actions or Records}}{\text{Total Number of Actions or Records}} \times 100$$

Where:

- **Number of Compliant Actions or Records** refers to the number of HR activities or records that are in compliance with relevant legal and regulatory standards (e.g., employment laws, safety regulations, data protection policies).

- **Total Number of Actions or Records** refers to the total number of HR activities or records tracked during the same period.

Employee-Led Resignation Rate:

The "Employee-led Resignation Rate" KPI tracks the percentage of employees who leave an organization voluntarily, typically due to personal reasons, career changes, or dissatisfaction with their job. A higher resignation rate can signal potential issues with employee engagement, company culture, or job satisfaction. Identifying trends in employee resignations can help HR teams address retention challenges, improve work conditions, and make adjustments to company policies or practices. By reducing employee-led resignations, organizations can minimize turnover costs and preserve institutional knowledge.

Formula for Employee-led Resignation Rate:

$$\text{Employee-led Resignation Rate} = \frac{\text{Number of Employee-Led Resignations}}{\text{Total Number of Employees}} \times 100$$

Where:

- **Number of Employee-Led Resignations** refers to the total number of employees who voluntarily leave the company due to resignation.

- **Total Number of Employees** refers to the total number of employees employed during the measurement period.

Hiring Process Satisfaction Rate:

The "Hiring Process Satisfaction Rate" KPI measures candidates' satisfaction with the company's hiring process, providing valuable insights into their experience during recruitment. This metric evaluates various aspects of the hiring journey, including job application ease, communication with recruiters, the interview experience, and overall professionalism of the process. A high satisfaction rate suggests that candidates find the process clear, efficient, and engaging, which can improve the company's reputation as an employer of choice. Conversely, a low satisfaction rate may indicate areas for improvement in candidate experience, such as overly complex application procedures or lack of timely communication. By tracking this KPI, organizations can fine-tune their hiring practices to ensure they attract top talent and provide a positive experience, which can also influence the candidates' decision to accept job offers.

Formula for Hiring Process Satisfaction Rate:

$$\text{Hiring Process Satisfaction Rate} = \frac{\text{Number of Positive Feedback Responses}}{\text{Total Number of Feedback Responses}} \times 100$$

Where:

- **Number of Positive Feedback Responses** refers to the number of candidates who rated the hiring process positively, typically through surveys or feedback forms.

- **Total Number of Feedback Responses** refers to the total number of feedback responses collected from all candidates who participated in the hiring process.

Cost per Hire:

The "Cost per Hire" KPI represents the total resources and financial investment required to acquire talent for the organization. This metric helps businesses assess the efficiency of their recruitment process by tracking how much it costs, on average, to hire a new employee. A high cost per hire could indicate that the recruitment process is inefficient or overly reliant on expensive methods like external agencies or job ads, while a lower cost suggests a more streamlined process. By monitoring this KPI, HR teams can evaluate whether their recruitment budget is being spent wisely, identify cost-saving opportunities, and refine hiring strategies to improve efficiency without sacrificing the quality of hires. Reducing the cost per hire can contribute to overall business profitability and enable more resources to be allocated to other areas like employee development and retention.

Formula for Cost per Hire:

$$\text{Cost per Hire} = \frac{\text{Total Recruitment Costs}}{\text{Total Number of Hires}}$$

Where:

- **Total Recruitment Costs** includes all expenses associated with the hiring process, such as advertising, recruitment agency fees, job fair participation, employee referral bonuses, recruitment software, interview costs, and HR personnel time spent on hiring.

- **Total Number of Hires** refers to the total number of employees hired during the period being measured.

Effectiveness of Training:

The "Effectiveness of Training" KPI measures the impact and success of a training program, specifically focusing on how well employees feel about the training and whether they perceive improvements in their performance as a result. For new hires, this metric is crucial to understanding whether the training provided adequately prepares them for their roles and responsibilities. A high effectiveness rate indicates that the training is aligned with employee needs, leading to higher performance and engagement. Conversely, a low effectiveness rate may suggest gaps in the training content or delivery, prompting HR teams to reassess and improve training methods or materials. By tracking this KPI, organizations can ensure that their training programs are not only well-received but also yield tangible improvements in employee competence, job satisfaction, and overall productivity.

Formula for Effectiveness of Training:

$$\text{Effectiveness of Training} = \frac{\text{Number of Employees Reporting Improved Performance After Training}}{\text{Total Number of Employees Trained}} \times 100$$

Where:

- **Number of Employees Reporting Improved Performance After Training** refers to the employees who self-report or are assessed as showing an improvement in performance after undergoing training.

- **Total Number of Employees Trained** refers to the total number of employees who participated in the training program.

Training Cost per Employee:

The "Training Cost per Employee" KPI quantifies the financial investment made by the organization in training, specifically measuring the average cost associated with onboarding and upskilling new hires. This metric helps businesses understand how much is being spent to ensure that employees, especially those new to the company, are equipped with the knowledge and skills necessary to succeed in their roles. A high training cost per employee may indicate a more intensive onboarding process or the use of specialized training methods, while a low cost could suggest more streamlined or less resource-heavy training programs. By tracking this KPI, organizations can assess the return on investment (ROI) for their training programs, identify cost-saving opportunities, and ensure that the training efforts are both effective and efficient in preparing new employees to contribute to the company's success.

Formula for Training Cost per Employee:

$$\text{Training Cost per Employee} = \frac{\text{Total Training Costs}}{\text{Total Number of Employees Trained}}$$

Where:

- **Total Training Costs** includes all expenses associated with training, such as the cost of training materials, facilitator fees, employee time spent in training, technology platforms, and any other related expenses.

- **Total Number of Employees Trained** refers to the total number of employees who participated in the training program, including new hires.

Percentage of Employees Trained:

The "Percentage of Employees Trained" KPI measures the proportion of employees who have completed training, providing insight into how well the company is equipping its workforce with the necessary skills and knowledge. Specifically, this metric reflects the rate at which new hires are being trained, ensuring they are prepared for their roles and aligned with company standards. A higher percentage indicates that a large portion of the workforce, including new employees, is receiving proper onboarding and skill development. On the other hand, a low percentage could signal gaps in the training program or inefficiencies in onboarding processes. By tracking this KPI, companies can evaluate the effectiveness of their training efforts, ensure that all employees are appropriately prepared, and identify opportunities to improve onboarding and development strategies for new hires.

Formula for Percentage of Employees Trained:

$$\text{Percentage of Employees Trained} = \frac{\text{Number of Employees Trained}}{\text{Total Number of Employees}} \times 100$$

Where:

- **Number of Employees Trained** refers to the total number of employees who have undergone training during a specific period.
- **Total Number of Employees** refers to the total number of employees within the company during that same period.

Diversity Rate:

The "Diversity Rate" KPI measures the percentage of employees in the organization who come from diverse groups. This metric is crucial for monitoring the success of efforts to create a diverse and inclusive work environment. A high diversity rate indicates that the company is effectively attracting and retaining employees from various backgrounds, fostering a workforce that reflects different perspectives and experiences. Tracking the diversity rate helps organizations assess the inclusivity of their hiring practices and work culture. A low diversity rate may signal a need for more proactive recruitment strategies or changes in workplace policies to create a more inclusive environment. By monitoring this KPI, companies can ensure they are on track to meet their diversity and inclusion goals, contributing to a more dynamic, innovative, and equitable workplace.

Formula for Diversity Rate:

$$\text{Diversity Rate} = \frac{\text{Number of Employees from Diverse Groups}}{\text{Total Number of Employees}} \times 100$$

Where:

- **Number of Employees from Diverse Groups** refers to the total number of employees who identify with diverse groups, such as gender, race, ethnicity, disability, age, or sexual orientation, depending on the organization's definition of diversity.
- **Total Number of Employees** refers to the overall employee count within the company.

Number of D&I Initiatives Implemented:

The "Number of D&I Initiatives Implemented" KPI reflects an organization's commitment to fostering diversity and inclusion (D&I) within the workplace. It tracks how many D&I programs or actions have been put in place to improve representation, inclusivity, and equality for employees from various backgrounds. A higher number of initiatives indicates a proactive approach to ensuring diversity and inclusivity across the organization. This KPI can include a variety of activities such as workshops, unconscious bias training, changes to recruitment practices, mentorship opportunities, and policy updates aimed at promoting a more inclusive and equitable work environment. By tracking this KPI, companies can assess their progress in creating a diverse workforce and workplace culture. It also signals to both current employees and potential hires that the organization is dedicated to diversity, equity, and inclusion, ultimately fostering a more positive, productive, and innovative organizational culture.

Formula for Number of D&I Initiatives Implemented:

Number of D&I Initiatives Implemented
= Total Count of D&I Programs Deployed

Where:

- **D&I Initiatives** refers to specific programs, actions, policies, or practices introduced to promote diversity and inclusion within the organization, such as training programs, recruitment initiatives, mentoring programs, employee resource groups, or policy changes.

- **Total Count** refers to the overall number of these programs or initiatives that have been successfully launched or completed within a given time period.

Average Time to Find and Hire:

The "Average Time to Find and Hire" KPI measures the efficiency of the hiring process by tracking how long, on average, it takes the company to fill an open position. It reflects the overall speed at which the HR department can identify, interview, and hire suitable candidates. A shorter average time to hire indicates a more efficient hiring process, with the ability to quickly identify and onboard qualified talent. On the other hand, a longer time to hire may suggest inefficiencies in recruitment, such as lengthy interview processes, unclear job descriptions, or slow decision-making. By monitoring this KPI, organizations can identify areas for improvement in their hiring processes, optimize recruitment workflows, and ensure that they are able to fill critical positions quickly to maintain business operations and growth.

Formula for Average Time to Find and Hire:

$$\text{Average Time to Find and Hire} = \frac{\text{Total Time to Fill All Vacancies}}{\text{Total Number of Hires Made}}$$

Where:

- **Total Time to Fill All Vacancies** refers to the sum of the time taken to fill each open position, measured from the moment a job is posted to the time the new hire accepts the offer and starts working.

- **Total Number of Hires Made** refers to the total number of new employees hired during the same period.

Acceptance Rate:

The "Acceptance Rate" KPI measures the success of an organization's recruitment strategies by evaluating the percentage of job offers accepted by candidates. A higher acceptance rate indicates that the company's job offers are attractive to potential hires, signaling effective recruitment practices, a competitive compensation package, and a positive candidate experience. On the other hand, a lower acceptance rate could point to issues such as inadequate compensation, a lack of alignment between candidates' expectations and the company's offerings, or shortcomings in the hiring process itself. By tracking this KPI, organizations can assess the effectiveness of their recruitment strategies and make necessary adjustments to attract and retain top talent. High acceptance rates also contribute to reduced time-to-fill and improved organizational stability.

Formula for Acceptance Rate:

$$\text{Acceptance Rate} = \frac{\text{Number of Job Offers Accepted}}{\text{Total Number of Job Offers Extended}} \times 100$$

Where:

- **Number of Job Offers Accepted** refers to the total number of job offers that candidates accept.
- **Total Number of Job Offers Extended** refers to the total number of job offers made to candidates.

Involuntary Termination Rate:

The "Involuntary Termination Rate" KPI tracks the percentage of employees who are terminated by the employer, whether due to performance issues, misconduct, layoffs, or other business-related reasons. This metric helps organizations assess the effectiveness of their retention strategies, performance management, and overall workforce stability. A high involuntary termination rate may indicate underlying issues such as poor employee engagement, ineffective management practices, or an unstable work environment, which could lead to increased turnover and reduced morale.

On the other hand, a low involuntary termination rate suggests that the company is able to retain employees effectively, addressing performance or behavioral concerns proactively. Monitoring this KPI allows businesses to identify trends, improve talent management practices, and take steps to create a more supportive and productive workplace culture.

Formula for Involuntary Termination Rate:

$$\text{Involuntary Termination Rate} = \frac{\text{Number of Involuntary Terminations}}{\text{Total Number of Employees}} \times 100$$

Where:

- **Number of Involuntary Terminations** refers to the number of employees who have been terminated by the employer, such as through layoffs, dismissals, or performance-related terminations.

- **Total Number of Employees** refers to the total headcount within the company during the same period.

Unlocking Business Success

For help with your HR Business needs, visit https://crystalcoasthr.com

or Contact Mike Arnold at

252-668-1640 at Crystal Coast HR.

www.ingramcontent.com/pod-product-compliance
Lightning Source LLC
Chambersburg PA
CBHW052200220526
45471CB00004B/1746